T0129475

You Must Learn NLP

156 WAYS LEARNING NEURO LINGUISTIC PROGRAMMING WILL IMPROVE YOUR LIFE

Dr. Heidi Heron PsyD & Laureli Blyth

BALBOA.
PRESS
A DIVISION OF HAY HOUSE

Balboa Press books may be ordered through booksellers or by contacting:

Balboa Press
A Division of Hay House
1663 Liberty Drive
Bloomington, IN 47403
www.balboapress.com.au
1 (877) 407-4847

Print information available on the last page.

ISBN: 978-1-5043-1132-8 (sc)
ISBN: 978-1-5043-1133-5 (e)

Balboa Press rev. date: 11/27/2017

This book is dedicated to our many teachers and students throughout the world. It is only with you that we can fulfil our passions to empower the lives we touch. Thank you.

Table of Contents

If you are reading this book, that means you are curious about Neuro Linguistic Programming (NLP). It is an intriguing topic after all! Perhaps you have worked with an NLP Coach or Therapist, or you've heard about it from someone, read a book, or maybe you've attended a workshop and your curiosity was piqued. So many people come to us after a glimpse into NLP and they want to know more! Whenever Tony Robins holds an event, we are flooded with inquiries!

As you will learn within these pages, NLP is a methodology and set of tools that can be used in all aspects of life. This book is a culmination of our blog of the same name: **You Must Learn NLP**. From decades of training, we are constantly explaining how NLP can be used, and we began the blog to answer these types of questions. The blog highlights the many uses and functions of NLP in personal development, communication, business, health, and with others, and it has become such a great tool that you are now fortunate to be holding it as a book.

We, your authors and trainers, have a great passion in sharing NLP through the world, helping to empower, enlighten, and enhance the world, one person at a time. Before we get too carried away, we want to introduce ourselves and share more information about *what* NLP is before you begin to learn *how* it can be used.

We are Laureli Blyth and Dr. Heidi Heron PsyD, owners and Principal NLP Master Trainers with the Worldwide Institutes of NLP (nlpworldwide.com), and it is a pleasure to share our world of NLP with you now.

Laureli started her journey in NLP in 1983 after attending a short workshop run by NLP Comprehensive in Colorado. She was working in the training department for United Airlines at the time and her NLP knowledge elevated her to new levels of skill and competency in training and interpersonal communication. After working corporately with her NLP skills, Laureli started the Australasian Institute of NLP in 1994, which is based in Sydney, Australia. She still runs her personal therapy and coaching practice and she trains NLP globally. Laureli also brings her background in esoteric sciences to NLP Worldwide, embracing fully the mind-body-spirit connection that NLP encompasses. Laureli is the founder of the Australasian NLP Association, author of *Neuro Intelligence* and co-author of *30 Days to NLP*. She is also a founding member of the NLP Leadership Summit.

Dr. Heidi began her NLP training in 1997 after participating in a weekend workshop with Robert Dilts and Robert McDonald in Sydney, Australia. She had been working in Human Resources and Operational Management at the time and began to implement her NLP knowledge into the workplace before starting her own NLP coaching, therapy, and consulting practice in 2000. At the same time, she joined Laureli as a Trainer at NLP Worldwide. She elegantly brings her higher education in psychology and communication, plus a Masters degree in Adult Education and Doctorate in Clinical Psychology into the fold of NLP. Dr. Heidi has held leadership positions on the Australian Board of NLP (Secretary and Chairperson) since 2006, is the co-author of *30 Days to NLP* and is on the Leadership team of the NLP Leadership Summit.

For more information about us, and to meet us via video introduction, please visit our website at **www.nlpworldwide.com/about-us**

Before we begin wanted to point out a few things about this book:

1. It is a culmination of blog posts: there are many simple articles that will share more about how you can use NLP. Because they are individual blog posts, you will read some of the same information over again, as each was written to be a stand-alone article.
2. Our writing style is very conversational vs. formal. What you are reading on the page is how we would say it in real life.
3. You can skip around. This is not a book written in a specific beginning, middle, and end format. If there is something you are interested in, go there!
4. The main function of this book is to pique your interest in NLP even more so you can make an educated choice about how you will use NLP when you decide to learn it more in-depth!

Okay, lets get started!

What is NLP?

Neuro Linguistic Programming (NLP) is a grouping of concepts, methodology, and skills to help you understand how the language of the mind creates the programs you run in life. The actual definition of NLP will vary from person to person, because as you will read in this book, NLP can be so many things.

What we'd like to do is take a few minutes to frame NLP and to give you some insight into the general history of NLP. Then we would like to begin sharing with you how you can personally benefit from learning NLP.

First, let's look at the basic descriptions of NLP:

> **Neuro:** The neuro of NLP deals with the mind and brain, but not just the brain that sits in your head. We are interested in all the neurology within your being: every cell, atom, chemical, hormone, and neurological connection.

> **Linguistic:** The linguistic of NLP has to do with your senses. We are interested in the verbal and non-verbal aspects of anything you can be aware of: what you see, hear, taste, touch, smell and think.

> **Programming:** The programming part of NLP is the most important. You have programming (or patterning) about everything you do; your beliefs, behaviours, actions, thoughts, and moods are based on the programming that you have.

Possibly, the real order of NLP should be, LNP—linguistic, neuro, programming—but it just doesn't sound as good! Everything that goes on around you is taken up **linguistically;** every single thing you've ever seen, said, tasted, touched, smelled, thought, or felt is within your awareness. Automatically, what has come into your awareness connects with your **neurology**; based on the internal or external stimuli, your brain creates and secretes chemicals, hormones, and neuro transmitters that instantly trigger your unconscious **programming** and you have a physical, mental, or emotional reaction. Instantly.

Let's look at a simple example. There may be a certain way a person can say your name that triggers an emotion from you. Here's what is happening:

1. You hear your name being said in a specific way (linguistic).
2. Your brain automatically creates and secretes a chemical based on what you've heard (neuro).
3. Your body immediately triggers an emotional reaction (programming).

So, NLP is understanding how the language of your mind creates the programs of your life. NLP also contains skills and knowledge that allow you to identify how the programs were created, how to enhance the programs that work well, and how to change what doesn't work well to be able to create the programming you desire.

As you will learn, you can use NLP to better communicate with others by learning more about how they have been programmed to understand, behave, and think. You can use NLP as a personal development tool to understand more about yourself, grow, change, and align your programming; in business you can use NLP to better understand and use the psychology of others; for your own health you can use NLP to align the mind/body connection; and you can use the skills of NLP as modality for helping others in all aspects of life, including as a Coach or Therapist.

Throughout this book, you will hear us talking a lot about the **conscious** and **unconscious** mind. The conscious mind is thought to make up only 10% of our mind. It is responsible for thinking, analysing, judging, and reasoning. While you may think it is your conscious mind that is in charge of you because you may be so aware of its incessant chatter, this isn't the case. Your **unconscious mind** makes up the other 90% of your mind. Also known as the subconscious or non-conscious mind, it is really this part of you that runs your body. It also stores your memories, creates your emotions, creates and transmits chemicals, and is responsible for every part of your life.

From an NLP perspective, It is your unconscious mind that we are interested in as this is the part of your mind responsible for storing and using your programs and patterns of emotions, thoughts, beliefs, and behaviours. If you've ever tried to logic your way into health or happiness, you'll know that your conscious mind isn't responsible for such things. It is your unconscious mind that we use in NLP.

A Brief History of NLP

It was through studying and eventually modelling a few specific therapists in the 1970's that connected the unconscious mind and its ability to be programmed and reprogrammed to the development of NLP as we know it today. Specifically, Fritz Perls, a Gestalt therapist, Virginia Satir, a family therapist, and Dr. Milton Erickson, a hypnotherapist, all obtained exceptional results with their clients and used specific techniques that worked and communicated directly with the unconscious mind. As you are undoubtedly aware of the plasticity of our brains, these therapists knew, understood, and used this concept before the term neuroplasticity was even coined.

Fascinatingly, the development of NLP happened quite by happenstance. The three official founders of NLP are Richard Bandler, John Grinder, and Frank Pucelik, plus there was a group of a dozen other people who were involved in the modelling and development of various concepts. This is the short story of how NLP was started, which will give you an insight into the minds and focus of the developers as you continue through this book.

Richard Bandler and Frank Pucelik were students at the University of California in Santa Cruz; it was a rather alternative university at the time, more focused on well-rounded education than specific majors. These two young men had been studying Gestalt Therapy with Fritz Perls before his death in 1970. Richard transcribed audio recordings of Fritz Perls and one day overheard Richard impersonating Fritz Perls with great accuracy. Richard also met Virginia Satir at a family reconstruction event, and he helped to transcribe the recordings of this training too. Similar to Fritz Perls, Richard was able to imitate Virginia Satir in such a way that he took on her body and voice characteristics. You see, Richard was a born modeller.

As senior students, Richard and Frank had the opportunity to teach a course at the university, and so they chose to teach a course on Gestalt Therapy. The requisite was a need for supervision of a staff member. Gregory Bateson introduced them to John Grinder, an Associate Professor of Linguistics, who became fascinated with the linguistic dance Fritz Perls used with his clients through Gestalt Therapy. Together, they all began unpacking the verbal and non-verbal toolbox of Fritz Perls.

At some point, Gregory Bateson introduced them to Milton Erickson, to study and learn the hypnotic linguistic patterns he used with clients. In a book written by Richard Bandler and John Grinder in 1975 entitled *Patterns of the Hypnotic Techniques of Milton H. Erickson, M.D.,* Milton wrote "In reading this book, I learned a great deal about the things that I've done without knowing about them."

From here, a group of about a dozen people began experimenting with aspects of all three modalities—Gestalt Therapy, family therapy, and hypnotherapy—creating tools, concepts, methodology, and processes that used the unconscious mind to identify what programming existed, how it was created, and how it could be changed. The first book about NLP, *The Structure of Magic*, was written in 1975 by Richard Bandler and John Grinder, and the development continued.

None of the core group were trained therapists, but they were curious enough to experiment with different concepts and learnings they gathered from Virginia, Frits, and Milton to create what we know today as NLP.

One of Richard Bandler's definitions of NLP is, "It's an attitude of curiosity and a methodology that leaves behind a trail of techniques."

Throughout this book, we hope you open to your own curiosity as you learn more about the methodology of NLP and how you can use these various techniques in all aspects of your life.

For a more in-depth explanation and introduction to NLP, we invite you to our free online intro to NLP at: **www.youmustlearnnlp.com/intro**

Now, let's open your mind to the wonder to the many ways learning NLP will benefit you.

Personal Development With NLP

"People don't really change, we just become more of who we truly are."

Dr. Heidi Heron

1. Learn That You are in Charge of Your Life

If there is one thing that NLP can do, it is empower people: empower them to be their best, be aware of the choices they make, take responsibility, and realise that each of us is in charge of our own lives.

Ultimately, we think this is something that most people already have a concept of, but with NLP as a framework, it begins to become blatantly obvious. How we live, the feelings we have, the actions we take—you are in charge of it all. You are not for your children, spouse, friends, or family—just you.

Through the original modelling that NLP did in the 1970's, the founders of NLP were able to unpack and understand how our programs of emotions, behaviours, beliefs, and thoughts are manifested and run by the unconscious mind. Your unconscious mind runs your body, stores your emotions, and runs your life in the background, much like your operating system of your computer or device.

When you begin to identify your programs (the ones that work well for you and the ones that don't), you will also gain understanding of how these programs were created by you. With this information, you can be empowered to fully step in and own the decisions you have made in your life, and you can be empowered to change patterns that do not serve you.

A woman we met recently regularly noticed a feeling of dread when she started to get emotionally close to people in her personal life. With some deeper questioning and exploration of this feeling, she identified it as a pattern of fear of being abandoned. It wasn't something she had been conscious of, but with further investigation, she became aware of a very old memory of when her baby brother was born and she took second seat. You see, we are always making decisions, acting in ways, and choosing based on our unconscious programming. Using NLP, we changed this program to fit her wants and desires in her current life. She was empowered to find understanding and make a change.

Not all the programs you identify are negative. Sometimes, using NLP, you will identify programs and the root of those programs that empower you to step more fully into a decision you made. A gentleman we worked with had a strong sense of self and confidence. He was interested in creating an anchor for these feelings so he could access these powerful states more consciously when he wanted to. Through a few simple NLP techniques, he accessed a past memory and decision he made many years ago. The memory was of a young boy (himself) who had just accomplished something and was given positive feedback from his father, something along the lines of "you are clever, aren't you," and he knew and believed if from that moment.

As a tiny baby and as an adult, we are making decisions, directing our lives and living in the best way we know how to, in the moment. With NLP, you will learn that each direction and step you take is your doing. Sure, other people may be influencers in your life, and they may help direct your choices, but at the end of the day, you are in charge.

Occasionally we hear remarks like "but, I have children that I *have to* take care of." *How* you take care of them is the choice you have and choice you take. Your children don't have to play sports on the weekends, go to the school they do, or eat the meals you cook, but they do those things because of the choices you are making. How well they play, study, or eat is up to them.

Sometimes, we *let* other people be in charge of us and that can sometimes feel like we are out of control. If you are in a relationship with someone who dominates you, or if you have beliefs that you aren't good enough, or perhaps you lack confidence—even if others take the lead in your life—you are still responsible for that programming, too.

NLP will help you to be more aware of the moments in your life and to embrace and rejoice in the wonderful moments and learn from the not-so-great moments. NLP will help you to re-evaluate the past, change your programming so you can respond more effectively, access resources so you can be more resourceful, change beliefs so you can life more aligned and ultimately not just realise that you are in control of your life, but *be* in charge of it.

There is a saying" "it's not what happens if life, it's how you react to it that matters," and NLP will help you to react in the way that is most effective and aligned for you.

2. Build Confidence

The confidence a person feels is an important factor in how they present themselves to the world. Generally, you have confidence about something that you do; for example, you might be confident that you can drive a car or confident in reading a book, or confidence in doing your job. On the other hand, if you are not quite skilled at something or if you have conflicting beliefs about your skills, you might have a lack of confidence. Examples of this may be: you don't feel confident that you could climb Kilimanjaro, or you may not be confident to run a marathon or write a book.

Sometimes a lack of confidence is based on a lack of skill, and rightly so. If I've never played the violin, I can't be confident in my skills of playing it. Sometimes however, a lack of confidence comes from a limiting belief, missing value, or other internal conflict.

To build confidence with NLP, you will first need to get specific on what kind of confidence it is and then identify what stops or blocks you from having confidence in that area of life. NLP contains many tools to help you to change beliefs, align values, and even clear conflict that may be standing in your way. You can even build or add extra resources you may need to boost your confidence, like self-belief, tenacity, resilience, or self-love.

Additionally, NLP is based on modelling. If there is an aspect in your life that you are confident about, we can map your confidence from that aspect of life onto another. This may come in handy if you lack the confidence to ask someone out on a date, but you have confidence to ask a stranger for directions.

You are in charge of your mind! So, when you get your mindset right about your confidence, anything becomes possible!

3. Regain Control of Your Life

Have you ever felt out of control or like you were no longer in charge of your life? Perhaps it felt like you were on a never-ending loop of sameness.

NLP has a presupposition that says **you are in charge of your mind and therefore your results**. With NLP, you can truly start to harness your life and be the leader, not just a participant.

Often, we find that when people feel out of control, they are either wandering through life without a plan or a goal, they are aimlessly following others hoping someone else has their answers, or they are holding onto the reigns of life so tightly they have gotten stuck and can't move forward.

Not only will NLP help you to identify what you want, but NLP will also help you to find out what is truly important to you, what is within your control, and help you to create a plan of action to create more success in your life.

Sometimes we have beliefs, emotions, thoughts, or other people in our life that hold us back. You will gain valuable tools to change and patterns which are not working in your favour so you can take back control of life. Sometimes we haven't yet given ourselves complete permission to be in charge.

When you can start to define what control means to you—both the positive and negative attributes of it—and you begin to be aware of what you want and what might be standing in your way, NLP will help you to easily bridge the gap and fully regain control in your life.

4. Enhance Your Self-love

The things we do for ourselves do not always result in self-love. In fact, sometimes they result in self-sabotage or self-confusion or self-doubt.

Most people do love themselves and evidence of this may show in the way they care for themselves. For instance, they get things like haircuts, clothes, holidays, cars, parties, drinks, as they seek and give love. In other words, they take care of their outer self. But they often neglect or even badly treat their inner self.

There is an NLP presupposition that says **every behaviour has a position intention**. Using NLP, you can discover the intention for the way you behave, respond, or act. This will allow you to find better ways of reaching your positive intention and getting it in alignment with what you truly intend. There are methods and tools to recover choice and change your behaviours and beliefs.

NLP also says that **you have all the resources to succeed.** These resources may not be apparent; in fact, they may be covered by negative thoughts or beliefs. So, when we learn how to recognize them and begin to use these resourceful gems our inner self begins to change. When you do this, you will find that balance and you will find the answers, attract love and esteem, balance, and harmony into your life, which will truly enhance your self-love.

5. Develop More Self-worth

Are you worthy? Have you ever felt unworthy? Worthy of what you may ask? Anything you desire! worthy of love, happiness, a great job, money, time, peace, freedom, a life well lived.

What if, as a newborn, you have all the self-worth you need? Think about it: a new-born child is not concerned about how much time, money, effort, or value they have. They don't have to *do* anything to receive love, food, care, shelter or clothing. They just have to *be*.

But, for some people, this changes overtime and the concept of self-worth becomes conditional. Conditional on doing a good job, getting good grades, being a good child, being quiet, helping others, or making someone else laugh or safe. Conditional self-worth can be detrimental in many ways; a person may create the need for external validation from others, a self-concept that is dependent on external factors or even a belief that they are simply not worthy of what was granted to us upon birth.

With NLP, you will be able to identify beliefs or conditions placed on your self-worth and create a change to these unconscious factors in life. If when you were born you didn't have to do anything at all to be worthy, what it be like if the same were true for you now?

You will be able to unharness any conditions to your self-worth and elevate your own worth to natural levels of being and worthiness. Just like when you were born!

6. Get to Know Yourself

How well would you say you know yourself? Interestingly, most your patterns of emotions, behaviours, and beliefs are largely unconscious— and are simply a part of what we do and how we act and how we behave. But, what if each and every thing you do is based on your programming? Would you know all those programs? Or do you think you live life on auto-pilot?

If you've ever heard anyone say something like "oh, that's just how I am," this is a loud alarm that really says, "I don't really know myself—I just do whatever happens and call it fate."

We tend to underestimate the importance of knowing ourselves. Many of us go through each day reacting to events and just getting by rather than making choices based on who we are and what we want. One of the most common remarks we hear from our students after they begin to learn NLP is "I truly understand and know myself more now—so now, I can respect my model of the world."

In NLP, this is a presupposition or assumption, to respect another person's model of the world. But, first and foremost, NLP will help you to understand and respect your own.

Your model of the world is made up of your history, memories, values, beliefs, concepts, imagination, and something we call meta programs, which are unconscious filters through which you make sense of your world. With NLP, you will learn not only more about what is important to you, what you believe, how your behaviours help or hold you back, but you'll also be able to figure out *why* you do what you do. You'll learn how to change what isn't working for you and enhance what is.

Unfortunately, not knowing yourself well can lead to confusion and wasting much time with indecision and second-guessing. However, when you know what motivates you, how to make better decisions, what is important to you, and how to change aspects that hold you back, something magical can happen. That something magical is that YOU can not only better understand yourself, you can become your own best friend!

7. Change Unwanted Habits and Behaviours

Have you ever had a habit or behaviour that you wanted to change? Maybe it was procrastination, or disorganisation, or being quick to anger. Or maybe it was more of a physical behaviour like smoking, biting your nails, or emotional eating.

You will learn how your unconscious programs lead directly to the behaviours you have in life, both the positive and negative behaviours. You will learn not just how to identify these behaviours and underlying patterns, but you'll also learn how to change these unwanted habits and behaviours.

The mind is very ritualistic in many ways, and works best with habits and routines; in fact, habits are very easy to create—but not always as easy to change! Often, we hear people say they continue with the old unwanted habit or behaviour because they don't know what they would rather do, they don't have the will power or resolve to change, or they tried but it didn't work.

We know that with NLP, if you have a strong enough desire, the *how* you make a change is easy. And, with some of the simple tools NLP has, you will be able to create quick and long-lasting changes to behaviours and habits that are no longer serving you. The longer-term benefit of this is that you will have practical tools that will help you to direct your thoughts, actions, and behaviours and ultimately have the power over your own life and mind.

With NLP, we have helped people change so many behaviours and habits in their lives. If something isn't working for you and if you want to change, you can use NLP! This might help you to quit smoking, putting yourself down, apologising unnecessarily, drinking too much, forgetting to put the lid on the toothpaste, driving too fast, reacting instead of being proactive, stop procrastinating, getting nervous, or any other behaviour that isn't in alignment with what you want in your life.

The first step is simply to choose which behaviour or habit to transform first!

8. Create New Behaviours

Whether you realise it or not, you are in a constant state of creation. The simple act of changing your job, home, or travelling or shopping in a new place creates a new behaviour. In fact, the brain is constantly changing or updating itself. It's always looking for better more beneficial efficient ways to operate. Carl Rogers called this the self-actualising tendency and what we now recognize as neuro-plasticity.

But what happens when you have a behaviour that seems to be ingrained and you really want it to change, but you can't?

The mere thinking about it does not create change by itself. Often to create a new behaviour you need to build a pathway to show and tell the brain/mind how to do it. In other words, create a new mental map in the brain and change the neuro-plasticity with conscious intention.

NLP was founded on modelling excellence and there are several powerful methods and modelling exercises that make a new behaviour easy and permanent. Some examples of new behaviours that can be created using NLP techniques are: being motivated, being proactive, being focused, being accepting, and being yourself. Many professional athletes, sports people, public speakers, actors, and singers use these tools to elevate and achieve their goals. Now anyone can learn how to do it for themselves using NLP.

9. Change Unresourceful Beliefs

Have you ever wondered why you do something, or why you behave in certain way, make certain choices or why life has turned out the way it has? The question "why" is probably the most asked question in the world. We humans are instinctively curious. Would you like the answer to this why question? Here it is:

You do what you do and how you do it because you have beliefs that support every decision you make.

Consciously or unconsciously, you have a belief about absolutely everything. And, if you think about your unconscious mind like a servant, it just follows orders from you. We have strong beliefs that we know about—I am a good person, I'm not good with money, I am successful, etc., —and we also have beliefs that lay below the surface and are less apparent in our lives, but probably more powerful.

According to Morris Massey, a Developmental Psychologist, between birth and the age of 7, we have very few filters in place and take in most of what we see, hear, and feel as truth. So, if we observe or overhear something (especially if it is from other who are important to us), our unconscious mind starts to code our beliefs, and our future is run off those beliefs.

Some unresourceful beliefs that some of our students have been able to identify and change include things like jealousy that was created when a new sibling was brought home, money limitations due to a father being out of work and the family struggling financially, weight gain because the parents told their child they were too little to handle the stress, slow learning style because they were told they were stupid as a kid, and fear, anger, and depression because of overseeing and overhearing adult conversations that had nothing to do with the person themselves.

With the skills of NLP, you will learn a variety of techniques to help you to identify and change any unresourceful beliefs you find. We know from an NLP standpoint, your unconscious mind works on the programming you provide it, and with the tools available you might as well provide yourself with the best programming you can!

10. Build Self-trust

Who do you trust more: a close friend or family member, or yourself?

As you think about that for a moment, we might even need to ponder a deeper question. What is self-trust? Is it self-confidence, reliance on yourself, faith in you? Perhaps, but maybe it's more than that. We believe that self-trust is the ability to rely upon your inner resources to navigate the world. Your inner resources include your emotions, physical body, and mental capacities. And it is most likely something that we learn over time.

We have met many people in the world with a low level of self-trust. When we inquire further about where this comes from, we learn a lot about this belief. And, it is simply a belief or a truth you hold about yourself. If you have self-trust or not, this belief is made up of your programming from past experiences and how you filtered what has happened.

Often adults we work with to build self-trust share with us experiences in the past where as children, their parents made all the decisions for them, the choices they did make were criticised, they did something that they were disciplined for, or they were told by someone else that they were not good at making decisions. Any of these things as a child or adolescent could shape the beliefs one holds about themselves.

When you can trust yourself, this leads to more positive self-esteem, positive regard for yourself, and confidence.

A few signs that you may not have a healthy level of self-trust might be a feeling of doubt when you are making a decision, always seeking external advice or endorsement before doing something, and/or a lack of confidence when it comes to following-through on something you want to do.

When you learn NLP, you will be more skilled to identify a pattern of self-trust within yourself and others. You will also gain NLP techniques that will assist you to clear or change patterns and beliefs that go with a low level of self-trust and you will learn to enhance the resources you do have while building your own trust in your ability to use these resources.

What would your world be like when you can not only trust yourself more, but you can truly rely on your inner resources to navigate your world in the best way possible? It will feel like magic.

11. Be More Flexible

How many ways are there to bake a cake? Make your bed? Approach conflict? Make a decision? Take care of yourself?

We have found that many people get stuck in their lives because they have only one or two ways to approach life. Humans are very ritualistic creatures and many of us like habit and routine to some degree, but if the practices we use aren't working well, something has to change.

One of the Presuppositions of NLP says **the person with the most flexibility will control the situation**, and another says **choice is better than no choice**.

With NLP, we want to create wholeness and choice through finding alternatives, choices, and options. If you happen to be a person who gets stuck because you keep trying to do something in the same way, it might be time to do something different! And, by that, we don't just mean something different through your behaviours! We mean changing your psychology!

As we write this, there are approximately 7.5 billion people on earth. That means there are at least 7.5 billion different ways of doing something. NLP will help you to find at least a few.

You will be learning and using NLP tools to help you to create a new perspective, generate a new behaviour, and change old patterns of emotions, behaviours, and thoughts. You'll also be addressing beliefs that may interfere with flexibility and creating a more flexible approach to life.

There is a great quote: **be stubborn about your goals and values, be flexible in your approach**.

12. Overcome Fears

Fears are a natural and important aspect to life; at their core fears exist to keep us alive. If you think of the 'flight or fight' mechanism that is built into all of us, this is generally triggered by a fear of sorts.

And while fears are a normal part of life and can be quite useful, they can also get in our way and prevent us from achieving what we truly want and desire. Many fears are mostly irrational. I can't think of a single case in history where someone has been killed by public speaking, for example!

Regardless of a fear being rational or irrational, NLP can assist you to overcome any fear that is holding you back. It might be a fear of public speaking, fear of not being good enough, fear of failure, fear of heights, spiders, dogs, mice, etc.; they can all be transformed using NLP.

Everything in our awareness (physical or mental) goes through a filtering process based on our history, beliefs, ideas, values, and concepts of life, and our brain automatically creates and secretes a chemical for everything. For fear, two main hormones are created and released: adrenaline and cortisol; the more chemicals released into your system, the stronger the fear will be.

Various NLP techniques will help you to address, change and re-evaluate past events, beliefs, values, ideas, and emotions to create a new neurological connection. This in turn changes the chemicals your brain creates and secretes. So, if a person did have a fear of public speaking, NLP could address the patterns of emotions, behaviours, and thoughts so that public speaking no longer triggers the reaction of fear!

A great thing to keep in mind when talking about fears is that you are in charge of your mind and therefore your results! If fear is not serving you in your life, you can change it.

13. Overcome Blocks and Limitations

Is there something holding you back from doing something or being someone you want to be? The patterns of emotions, behaviours, beliefs, and thoughts that seem to run us and create some of the blocks and limitations that we hold on to are created and generated by the unconscious mind.

As coaches, if someone comes to us and says, "Can you help me remove a block of X?" our question is, "Do you know what you want instead or what you'll be able to do without X?" and if they have a positive answer, that is, they know what they want instead or they know what life will be without the block or limitation, then our answer is," Yes."

One of the key factors in overcoming any block or limit in our life is to have an imagination vivid enough to picture life without it. This becomes your Desired State and what we are working toward. With a goal to achieve in mind, you can then start to apply some specific NLP skills that will help to access and clear the root cause, anchors, change unconscious processes, create new beliefs, new patterns, and ultimately not just overcome, but remove blocks and limitations that may have held you back in the past.

14. Remove Feelings of Helplessness and Hopelessness

Often patterns of depression or worthlessness include feelings of being helpless and hopeless; these are definitely not useful, resourceful, or particularly nice feelings to have. A great thing we know from NLP is that you haven't always felt this way.

When we meet a person who is feeling helpless or hopeless, not only do we want to know if there are any internal or external factors that have created these feelings so we can alleviate or remove these factors, but we also want to know when you have felt good.

Your unconscious mind stores the blueprints of the perfect you in body, mind, and spirit. It also is the storehouse for every single memory that you have ever, ever, ever had, and with those memories comes emotions that create a cellular connection to chemicals, hormones, and positive reactions. Therefore, by using NLP, you can tap back into and restore neurological connections of your desired state, whether that is happiness, freedom, peace, or simply feeling at ease.

Feelings like hopelessness and helplessness are not ones that you have to live with. NLP will help you to reconnect with more resourceful and positive emotions and will help you to clear, change, and reassess any past experiences that have created these feelings to surface in the first place.

15. Create More Success

We are sure you're successful already, which is what you should be! But what if you could really get to know yourself in a way that would help you to create even more success in your life?

With NLP, you will learn about your unconscious filters which connect directly to your success strategies. Some of these include your motivational drivers, what you are pulled toward or pushed away from, compelling instincts of counting or discounting, patterns of flexibility, emotional intelligence, and more.

We know that when you know better, that allows you to do better. So, not only will you be learning more about what makes you tick, but we will also be identifying anything that might hold you back from creating success in your life, such as limiting beliefs, behaviours, self-talk, etc.

NLP also contains tools to help you to identify and create goals, along with a plan of action to take steps to achievement, all while managing your state and psychology. You probably already have some ideas of what success means to you; with NLP, you can bring even more of that into your life!

16. Create Goals and a Pathway to Achieving Them

How do you create goals? When we ask most people, they tell us that they figure out what they want and then start working toward it. Most don't write it down, tell anyone else, create a plan, or really associate into their goals. So, if you already do any of that, you are ahead of the game!

In NLP, we have a step-by-step tool called the **Well-Formed Outcome;** it is a strategy that uses mainly aspects of your unconscious (non-thinking) mind to identify, connect with, and strategize the achievement of a goal. It is a formula that encapsulates emotion, visualisation, steps, and even what is known as an evidence procedure.

A great tool you will learn with NLP is the **Meta Model**, which are questions to help create more specificity and take out the ambiguous elements to a conversation or a thought. With the use of these questions with the Well-Formed Outcome, you are learning how to not just create a goal, but structure it in such a way that the unconscious mind is compelled to be drawn toward it and away from what life is like without this goal.

The unconscious mind is a miraculous tool, and the more you understand how yours is programmed, you can use your programming and strategies to make achieving your goals even easier now.

17. Discover the Goals Behind Your Goals

Most people are motivated by having a goal, one that is attainable, achievable, and worthwhile to them.

These 'background' words—attainable, achievable, worthwhile (or whatever your specific words might be)—are part of the **meta goal** of your goals. "Meta" is a Greek word that means *beyond* or *above*, so your goal of your goal. Everything we do has some sort of intention or benefit for us, or secondary gain if you will. If you have a goal that is attainable, achievable, and worthwhile, whatever it is, achieving this goal creates a sense of achievement, satisfaction, self-confidence, self-belief, and many other by-products.

By discovering the *hidden agenda* behind your goals this can help you to become even more motivated, determined, and focused on achieving your goals. And, while we always have invisible meta-goals like we just talked about, there are often more obvious meta-goals.

For example, a person who wants to step up in their profession and job and seek an advancement or promotion may have additional meta-goals such as the promotion giving them more money, the money provides more stability,

stability provides a sense of security and security can lead to higher self-confidence to attract a partner into their lives.

Or, recently, we worked with a person who wanted to write a book and her goal behind this goal was to become a motivational speaker on the speaking circuit. Sometimes it just takes a spark from one goal to create the momentum for the next. By understanding the internal or external goals beyond your goals, you'll have an even bigger spark to create from.

18. Develop a State of Being 'In the Flow'

When you are in a state of flow, is it like time stands still? Does it sometimes feel everything else has stopped except for what you are doing in that moment? Or maybe, the state of flow is a new one to you, something that others can achieve but is so far illusive to you?

When we are talking about states from an NLP perspective, we are talking about a mood or emotion. The state of flow, a term coined by Positive Psychologist Mihaly Csikszentmihalyi (pronounced chic-sent-me-high) is a state of complete absorption with the activity or situation you're involved in. It is a state in which people are so involved in an activity that nothing else seems to matter. Some people call it being "in the zone" or "in the groove." Everyone experiences it at some point and describes it using phrases like: a feeling of great absorption, engagement, fulfillment, and skill, and during which concepts of time, food, self, etc., are typically ignored.

In fact, while in a total state of flow at an airport, sitting at the gate, I missed a flight! They were even calling my name! I've now put in measures to stop that from happening!

So, now that you know more about what it's like to be in the flow, what does NLP have to do with it?

Anything you want!

With your NLP skills, you will be able to create an anchor which will trigger your state of flow anytime you want. An anchor is a stimulus that creates a response. For me, I've created an anchor using the word 'now,' and that word (and how I say it) triggers a feeling like a cone of silence coming down around me, and I have total focus and concentration on what is happening *now*.

Since the airport incident, I have adapted it to have my unconscious mind check in every few minutes to my immediate surroundings to attend to anything I need to, and I have also chosen to never use it in a situation where I may be needed to respond, such as getting on an airplane!

When you choose to use your anchor, and help yourself create the flow state, there will be nothing that can get in your way!

19. Model Success from Yourself

What is something that you do well? It may be something simple or intricate, such as how you connect with people, organise a party, talk to people you don't know, make a meal, anything! From NLP, we know this: you do something well because you have beliefs and unconscious programs that uphold and create this success. And if you do something well in one area of your life, using NLP, you can unpack the beliefs, programs, and strategies to map across to another area of life.

Fantastically, NLP contains many tools to help you to unpack your unconscious patters and model this success. Most often, modelling is thought of as a tool to 'model others,' however, we have found that one of the first places to start when it comes to modelling success is within you.

You might find that you want to improve your ability to connect to new clients at work, and you may have the simple ability to connect with friends. You already have the psychology to meet and connect with people easily; you can unpack that and create the same psychology at work. Or, you might want to create a more organised style in your work or home life, and you find that you can organise a party or events easily. Again, we can unpack this pattern and install it within a different context.

There is a great NLP Presupposition that helps to understand this concept: if you can spot it, you've got it. The first step is identifying what area of your life contains a behaviour, attitude or mindset you want to use in a different area of life—then, the NLP fun begins!

20. Model Success From Others

There is so much goodness in others; the way someone solves a problem, finds time to do everything they desire, how people keep their cool in stressful situations, even how they communicate with others, and themselves.

Here's another cool thing: if someone else does something, you can do it, too!

NLP is based on **modelling,** that is, studying how something or someone works. By observation, association, and understanding the underlying patterns of thought, behaviour, emotions, and beliefs, you can identify and learn how you can do what they do.

For example, maybe you admire how someone at work has such an easy ability to talk to just about anyone and make a strong connection quickly. You could model that. NLP even has a tool or strategy that you can use to understand others and get their model.

In general, if you have time to sit with another person and have a conversation, you could easily identify their values, beliefs, internal dialogue, physiology, and unconscious filters they use when doing what you want to model. You can then take what fits for you and take it into your life. If you don't have the ability to be with someone in real life (maybe you want to model Oprah, but you don't know Oprah), you could use the same tool and strategy to identify your perceptions of what she does on a mind or psychological basis; either will work.

We like to identify people who have redeeming traits and qualities that we would like to have ourselves or that we would like to share with our students and we ask to interview them and model them. Ultimately, there is no bigger sense of flattery than being asked to be modelled!

Who do you want to model?

21. Be an Inspiration to Others

Here is a quote that we love: **the way you do anything is the way you do everything**.

Finding people in the world who live their best life is often hard to find; unfortunately, so many people put up with living mediocre lives and not doing enough to make their lives as successful as they could be.

This world needs more inspirational people, that is, people who walk their talk. This is something to be admired and respected, and doesn't happen enough! With NLP, you will have more tools available to you to help you know when you are incongruent, gain sensory acuity internally and externally to assist you in identifying areas to improve within yourself, your workplace or your life in general, and you can be a role model by inspiring others to live their life congruently and authentically too.

NLP will not make you perfect! It will help you be a better human. And humans are flawed! We have bad behaviours, we have emotional outbursts, we don't always make the best choices. And that in itself *is* perfect! As an NLPer, we know that it is our unconscious patterns that drive us, and if something isn't working, we have the tools to address it, change it, fix it, and at least understand it.

Our wish for everyone learning NLP is to embrace the tools, skills, and concepts of NLP, first and foremost for yourself, so you can live the best life you can, and be an inspiration to others to do the same.

22. Identify and Improve Your Learning Strategy

How did you learn how to learn? Did you take a class? Read a book? Did your parents sit down with you when you were little and take you step-by-step though a process of learning?

Yeah, us neither.

We don't *learn* how we learn, we *just learn*.

Wouldn't it be great to be able to unpack your learning strategy and tweak it to make it better and be able to access it and use it anytime you want to learn anything you want easily?

Guess what? NLP can help with that.

With NLP, you will be able to find your own learning strategy through understanding the unconscious filters you use to learn (called Meta Programs), identifying the eye accessing cues you use when you learn and by uncovering any beliefs that may be hindering your learning success. By understanding how and why you learn the way you do, you'll be able to improve your strategy, even model someone else on the way they learn, and you'll be able to replicate your strategy anytime you want to learn something new.

So, while you never learned how to learn, you can teach yourself now!

23. Improve Your Memory

We've heard a lot of people tell us things like "I have a bad memory," "I can't remember anything," "I have very poor recall," or other similar un-resourceful belief statements. Our first couple of questions when we are told this is, "Compared to whom?" and, "How do you know?"

When people believe they have a bad memory, they usually do. But which came first, the belief or the bad memory? Most likely it is the belief.

Often, people create beliefs about themselves by doing a comparative analysis, not with specific people, but with a concept they have in their mind. In other words, they are not actually comparing themselves with other people but what they think they *should* remember.

It has been said that 10% of our mind is the conscious mind—this is the thinking, analytical, reasoning, and critical thinking part of our mind—and 90% of our mind is the unconscious mind. The unconscious mind is where all our memories are stored, and it is thought that we have access to as little as just 3% of this part of our mind. Regardless of if you remember something, your unconscious is the storehouse for all memories, emotions, concepts, feelings, behaviours, and everything else that has ever happened in your life.

Think about your unconscious mind as a large and deep pond. If you drop a coin into the pond, you may not be able to see or access it, but you know that it is there. This is the same for the unconscious mind. It contains millions of coins from your life, and through a variety of techniques from NLP, you'll be able to access those coins, or memories, with ease.

In today's world, there is so much to keep track of. And, if you are getting yourself off to work, the kids off to school, and you are remembering where you live at the end of the day, you're doing pretty good! But, in all seriousness, most 'bad memories' out there are a result of unsupportive beliefs.

Luckily, NLP can help with that! Not only will you be able to challenge some beliefs, but you will also learn how to trust your unconscious mind more effectively, put in place some strategies to help with memory recall, and ultimately, improve your memory.

24. Manage Your Mood

When it comes to your moods, are you more proactive or reactive?

Makes you think, doesn't it? Of course, I think we'll like to believe that we are more proactive about the moods and emotions that we have, but in truth we are reactive. It's just how we are programmed.

You see, everything that is your conscious and unconscious awareness can trigger your mood and emotions, and I mean everything—even the things that you are not consciously aware of. Perhaps *especially* the things that you are not consciously aware of.

The **NLP Communication Model** explains what happens in the mind that makes us reactive to what is going on around us. The Communication Model says that as we go about our daily life, our unconscious mind is automatically filtering through what we are bringing in through our five senses; what we see, hear, taste, touch and smell, even what we think to ourselves. Our mind is filtering this information based on our beliefs, ideas, culture, bias, decisions, patterns, gestalts, and more. Once we filter it, the unconscious mind makes it fit into our schema of the world by distorting, deleting, and generalising information. All of this happens in an instant.

Immediately, our unconscious mind creates some sort of internal representation of the moment by way of an internal movie, sound, or feeling, and we react chemical and neurologically to this by the production of chemicals and hormones which are directly secreted into our body, resulting in a state change. A state, simply put, is a mood or emotion.

So, to answer the question asked earlier: when it comes to moods, you are more reactive. From there, we can be proactive, and NLP will help you to become more proactive by helping you to identify and change some of the filtering you automatically do, which leads to your moods. For example, if you know that get sad or depressed on cloudy days, wouldn't you rather alter the state that these types of days have on you? Or if you get angry when someone gives you feedback, wouldn't you rather be receptive and open?

To create any change with NLP or any other tool, you must first be aware of what reactions you are having and then you can be proactive about creating an alternative reaction. When you learn NLP, you will become more aware of the moods and emotions that you exhibit in different situations. Most of the time, you'll probably find that your auto-pilot is working just fine. In the instances where you see that an improvement could be made, this is where you will bring in your change tools and state management awareness.

One of the things we love about NLP is that it helps us to be more aware, proactive, and in charge of our mood, emotions, and outcomes in life.

25. Anchor States of Excellence

If you could instantly access a specific state or emotion, what would it be? Would you choose calmness, motivation, strength, confidence, or an unstoppable personal power? Where would you use it?

And, what if you didn't have to choose just one state; rather, you could create a way to instantly access any state you wanted, and access that as easily as the click of your fingers? Just. Like. That.

Well, with NLP you can! If you've been around NLP for a while you will have heard of anchors. If you're new, let me explain. An **anchor** is a stimulus that triggers a response. Much like Pavlov's dog began to salivate at the sound of a bell, you can create an anchor for yourself (or many) that will trigger any state you desire.

You already have a variety of anchors that have been naturally created overtime. Perhaps there is a song that puts you into a certain mood, or a smell. Maybe you automatically react in a certain way when you see something specific or if someone says your name in a certain way. These are all anchors—a stimulus that creates a response—and NLP has unpacked how the mind specifically creates these anchors so we can purposefully use this unconscious mind technology.

In fact, when you learn NLP, you will learn how the mind responds at peak situations when a stimulus can be applied to create an anchor. When you create an anchor that will be resourceful for you, we call this a **resource anchor**. You'll be able to create anchors for yourself and other using specific words, a touch (think of Tony Robbins chest pump and you'll see a dynamic anchor in action), a sound, a song, a picture, a smell, really just about any stimuli. And you can anchor nearly any feeling you want. You can even stack different resources with the same stimulus so there is a cascade of emotions present when you set the anchor off.

Because you are in charge of your state management and the mood you are in at any given point, anchors allow you to be even more mindful and in control of your state and mood. Next time you want to ask someone on a date, trigger your confidence anchor. When you want to fall asleep easily, use your relaxation anchor. When you want to go to the gym, access your state of motivation easily.

After all, you are in charge of your mind, aren't you?

26. Collapse Old Anchors

When we are talking NLP language, an anchor is a stimulus that creates a response. For example, a certain song might create a happy or a sad response. The smell of roses might take you back to your wedding day. The sunshine might trigger a sense of happiness and a stormy day may trigger sadness or withdrawal.

Ultimately, anytime you have a conditioned response occur, that is an anchor.

Sometimes, the responses we have do not serve us in a beneficial way. If, for example, something triggers fear or depression or anxiety, you might be better off without that anchor. In fact, most fears we have (fear of dogs, public speaking, failure, heights, flying, etc.), in their basic element, are an anchor of some sort.

NLP contains tools that will help you to collapse old anchors, diffusing them so they no longer affect you. So, the dog no longer creates fear, you can feel happy on a stormy day, the baby crying no longer makes you angry, and neither does the bad driver you are behind on the road!

NLP can not only help you to collapse anchors that are not serving you, but it can also help you change these old patterns of thought and action to help set you up for a new desired state.

27. Change How You Respond to Your Internal Dialogue

Everyone has internal dialogue going on most of the time; this is the soundtrack of your thoughts. The difference between someone who gets overloaded with their own thoughts and someone who does not is simply what they pay attention to.

NLP will provide you with sound techniques that *help* turn off that overactive mind and find more practical ways to know what to pay attention to. While we are *always* thinking, the aim is to let the background chatter be just that; background chatter.

NLP understands that the same neural pathways are used for thoughts and spoken language and your body responds the same to both. Therefore, when we experience negative thoughts or words from others, our mind responds the same way. Even written language produces the same neural pathways to be used. And, if you respond negatively to these messages, the unconscious mind will often create a sensation in the body (often tension or pain); this sensation in turn sends a message back to the brain and a loop of negative thinking begins to run and the same patterns in the brain and body get triggered chemically, emotionally, and behaviourally.

The good news? NLP will teach you to become familiar with your own patterns so that you can be aware of and map out where your thinking tends to lead. You will be able to also address any beliefs, behaviours, and unconscious filters that may exist due to past events, trauma, or a lack of stability or safety.

When you know better, you can do better and learning to manage your internal thoughts is a life-changing skill that everyone should know and learn to use.

28. Create More Positivity

You know that 'glass is half full' type of person? It would be nice to *be* her every now and then, wouldn't it? Maybe not all the time, but more often than having the pessimistic mindset.

Yes, mindset. Positivity is a mindset.

In NLP, our frame of reference, or how we see our world (in NLP speak, our Model of the World) is created by our mindset. We filter what is happening in our world through a lens of our beliefs, values, and meta programs, which are the very unconscious elements of our mindset.

With NLP, you will learn how to identify these lenses of yourself and others and how to change them if you want.

Often, when we meet people who want to have more positivity in their life, we find that their mindset normally does the following: they look at the problems versus the desired results, they move away from what they don't want instead of toward what they want, they discount the good instead of collecting it, and/or they generalise and hypothesize about what might possibly go wrong.

Excitingly (which is already positive!), with NLP we can begin to change and reshape beliefs and these meta-programs through a variety of NLP tools. This helps to create a psychological mindset change—thus bringing in more positivity into your life!

29. Increase Motivation and Drive

In moments where you lack motivation and drive, what do you do? Most people will wait around for motivation to come, like it is a bus or a train. But what if motivation and drive weren't actually a *thing* to attain or wait for, but rather a state of mind?

What if in moments where you lack motivation and drive, you could tap into your resources and *access* the motivation and drive you desire? What would happen then? Most likely you would do more, achieve more, and possibly even *be* more. At the very least, it would allow you more choice in life, and the ability to create motivation or not.

The study of NLP understands that motivation and drive are states of the mind. A state is a mood or emotion that you are having at any given moment because of the immediate circumstances. NLP also knows how you can consciously create a state when it is needed or desired.

Your states—all of them, not just motivation and drive—are created because of the beliefs, unconscious filters, memories, and decisions that you have made during your life. If motivation isn't present when you need it, that is simply because the right criteria (beliefs, filters, etc.) are not aligned in that moment. However, you can change that.

When you learn NLP, you will first be introduced to a great tool called the **well-formed outcome;** this tool is used to create clarity about a goal or outcome. When you are clear about what you want with a deliberate plan of action, motivation is always more readily available. Anytime you are feeling overwhelmed, unclear, or unsure about something, motivation will wane.

Next, you will utilise strategies from NLP to manage your state. By stepping into and accessing past experiences of motivation and drive, your body will begin to reassociate into this state, creating and secreting chemicals through your body that will amplify a motivational state. Sometimes **acting as if** is a great way to kick-start motivation. When you act *as if* you are motivated, the mind/body connection reacts *as if* you are motivated; thus, motivation ensues.

Finally, you will gain a variety of tools from NLP to help you model the motivation and drive of others and yourself. You will be able to use a process called **new behaviour generator** to model someone else and you'll also be able to dig deeper into the unconscious mind and begin to understand the **meta programs** (unconscious filters) that you and others use in times of motivation. These tools will again allow you to act as if, but in a more robust manner.

If something is possible for you or another person at some point in time, it is possible at any time. Motivation and drive are not concepts to *wait* for; they are states you can access whenever and wherever you desire.

30. Find Your Passion

Do you know what you are passionate about? What you love? What you enjoy? We hope so. But, we also know that so many people get caught up in the day-to-day aspects of life that they miss the passion aspect of life.

Is it imperative to know what your passions are? No, probably not—but it helps when you're looking to increase your levels of happiness and flow in life. We're not talking about passions that you can create into workplace activities necessarily, but passions you can indulge in as a past time or with friends or even in the workplace.

We've found too many people who think they need to find a passion and then find work within their passion. But, that doesn't always work out. If you have a passion for knitting, you might not actually be able to create a sustainably paying job to just knit. Or perhaps you're passionate about helping others;

you may or may not be able to land the perfect job to help you do that. But, when you can find your passions and find out how to add them into your life—even with your current job or situation—you will be more fulfilled, whole, and happy!

With NLP, you will learn to identify your values, motivational strategies, and patterns which make your heart sing. When you know this information, you can use it to channel into your life, tap into your passions, and create even more greatness in your day!

31. Find Your Purpose

What is your purpose? Are you supposed to have one? Does everyone have one? How would you know if you found it?

These are questions that clients ask a lot when it comes to finding their purpose. And we don't know the answers to any of these questions.

But you do.

When you learn NLP, you will be developing a strong sense of rapport with your unconscious and higher conscious mind. It is your higher conscious mind that truly knows your purpose and mission in life. This is the *all-knowing* part of your mind; some people call it the greater whole, or collective unconscious, or universal consciousness, or even spirituality. And, some people don't believe in it because they can't see or feel it.

Through understanding yourself, connecting with your higher self, trusting your unconscious mind, and truly getting to know you, you will find answers for yourself about what is important for you, what you believe, how you get motivated, and how you fit best in your world.

From NLP, some people have found their purpose is in helping others, or solving a problem, or creating a solution. Some have identified their purpose is to raise their children the best they can, spread a positive message, or shed light for the world. We've met people who have come to their own understanding that their purpose in this life is simply to be happy.

Regardless of who you are, where you are, or what you've been doing with your live, NLP will help you to better understand you and help you to find your purpose!

32. Enhance Your Choices

NLP allows people to have more choices about their lives. Richard Bandler, one of the founders of NLP, says, "Most of all, NLP is about freedom."

NLP is an extremely powerful set of techniques for rapid and effective behavioural modification. It is said by many to contain the most accessible, positive, and useful aspects of modern psychology, and can be helpful in virtually every aspect of personal and inter-personal relationships.

NLP can help you to achieve effective communication, increase self-awareness, create new behavioural responses, and adapt them to achieve more choices and success. It enables you to add flexibility and effectiveness to your work and personal life, and improve the quality and range of your life choices.

One of the aspects in making choices is to know what you want or what is your intention or outcome. Many people do not have conscious outcomes and wander randomly through life. NLP stresses the importance of living with conscious purpose or intention and therefore has several methods and techniques to getting the mind uncluttered and clear and making choices that are in alignment with what it wants. NLP is about thinking, observing, and doing to get what you want out of life and this requires the ability to increase your choices.

33. Create a Connection with Your Higher Self

Have you met your higher self? Your higher self is your all-good, all-knowing, all-powerful self. No, we're not talking about God, but it may be in similar likeness.

Now, NLP doesn't have a spiritual foundation and some schools of NLP do not look at the concept of a higher self. But with NLP Worldwide, we do. We believe that a person is much more than a mind and body; we also have a spiritual connection. Call it what you will, but we believe there is something bigger, more powerful, and more purposeful than just our mind and body.

With NLP, we think of you as having three minds: the **conscious**, **unconscious**, and **higher conscious** mind. The **conscious** mind is responsible for thinking, analysing and reasoning. The **unconscious** mind is what we are interested in from an NLP perspective; it is the storehouse of all memories and emotions, and it runs your body, keeps you safe, and is the starting place for all your programming. Your **higher conscious** mind is outside of all of this, and it is responsible for things like intuition, knowingness, ethereal awareness and a connection with something more than us as human beings.

Many people have an idea that their higher conscious and higher self exists, but they don't have a way to tap into it. Some people don't believe it because they don't have any proof of its existence. And other people have a strong connection that they rely on, trust, and connect with regularly.

NLP has quite a few tools that will help you to build a relationship with your higher self. It has always been there, but sometimes we don't know how to connect to it. Using a few techniques from NLP, you can create an open loop of communication from your higher conscious mind to your unconscious mind to your conscious mind.

Being more open, connected, and responsive to your higher self has many benefits. To name just a few: you will develop a stronger sense of intuition, your soul's purpose will become clearer, answers to your questions will be more easily found, you'll be more in control of your happiness, you will have more self-love, more authentic connection with yourself, and you'll never be alone.

Through the years, one of our favourite moments of working with NLP is when someone is connected and meets their higher self for the first time. It is magical to watch, and an absolute delight and joy to experience. Have you met your higher self yet?

34. Change Old Childhood Patterns

According to Dr Morris Massey, a developmental psychologist, the majority of the beliefs, behaviours, habits, and values we run as adults were actually generated during the *imprint* period of life between birth and 7 years old.

There is a very good chance that some of your anger, anxiety, self-doubt, optimistic viewpoint, resilience, and strength were influenced by childhood experiences. We learn from those around us, so it makes sense that some aspects of us would be based on our past. But, does that mean we are stuck with these aspects of ourselves for the rest of our lives?

Luckily, no. NLP can be a wonderful way to change old childhood patterns that may not be serving you now.

Recently, we worked with a woman who had a fear of failure. This would show up in her life as not feeling good enough, needing to be perfect, and worrying about what other people would think.

NLP will teach you how to have more insight into how people (including yourself) think, respond, and behave. With this understanding, you can apply various techniques that will help to uncover beliefs, strategies, and unconscious patterns that were developed in childhood (or elsewhere for that matter!)

With our client who had a fear of failure, we utilized an NLP process that includes access to your timeline of history and events which have contributed to who you are today. This woman found a memory of being a small girl and overhearing her parents talking about her being uncoordinated in her dance class. She recalled feelings of failing, not getting it right and not being good enough; and that began a pattern he lived with for another 30+ years!

Think about that for a moment. She overheard people talking to each other about her and decided to make a decision about failure and perfection to last the rest of her life. A few things here: 1) they may not have been talking about her specifically, 2) she maybe hadn't yet developed coordination skills, and 3) she may not have actually failed in any way!

An NLP presupposition that we often filter through is **you are doing the best you can with the resources you have available**, and as a young kid, she was doing the best he could! With this NLP technique, detached her from a few old beliefs that about failure, being good enough and needing to be perfect.

Consider for a moment the possibility of changing childhood patterns. And being able to do this by empowering yourself to be more resourceful and in control over your life and how you perceive the past. What patterns would you change?

As one of the founders of NLP, Richard Bandler, says, "When using NLP, it's never too late to have a happy childhood."

35. Forgive Yourself and Others

When it comes to forgiveness, we have two favourite quotes: "I don't forgive because I am weak, I forgive because I'm strong enough to understand that people make mistakes," and, "When you forgive you heal and when you let go you grow."

Have you ever had a hard time forgiving someone? It's hard work! To hold on and be unforgiving means that somewhere in your conscious awareness you must hold onto whatever wrong was done in the past; you must remember it to hold on. The emotional toll this can take on the body is amazing. We have seen so many health-related issues come about because they were unable to forgive.

One of the objections we often hear to forgiveness is the person who was hurt doesn't want to forget. They think that forgiving means forgetting and accepting a wrong that was done to them in the past. It doesn't have to mean that at all. In fact, the best type of forgiveness is a *forgive and remember*, but instead of remembering the hurt, remember the lesson. Remember you've been through that experience and you don't have to relive it over and over again.

That's what happens when you are unable to forgive; you relive the experience over and over again The act of forgiveness releases the cellular memory so you can finally move on and move forward. You can be empowered by forgiving others.

When you are being unforgiving of yourself, self-forgiveness is the ultimate act of love and compassion you can have toward yourself. When you are unable to forgive yourself for something (a decision or behaviour from the past), you are holding yourself in the prison of your mind and you are not allowing yourself to learn from your past and move into the future. In fact, you are reliving the experience and projecting that continuously into your future.

NLP can help you to forgive yourself and others in a few ways. First, you will learn that NLP often looks for the *positive intention* behind any behaviour: the benefit for another person to have done something. Generally, there will be a positive intention for any act; understanding this does not mean you approve of the behaviour, but you can start to understand the motives or hidden agenda behind the painful behaviours. Secondly, NLP advocates separating a person and their behaviour; we all have a myriad of different behaviours, and none of them singularly define us. Having a frame that people are not their behaviours helps us to dissociated from the situation, possibly even to a new point of view helping us to forgive.

Additionally, NLP contains many tools to tap into the unconscious beliefs and programming around forgiveness. You will learn techniques that will help you to reframe, realign, and change decisions that you made to hold on and be unforgiving. You will also learn how to dissociate from past experiences and change the submodality coding to code them as old beliefs and memories, instead of present and happening now. Furthermore, you will gain tools that will allow you to release the cellular memory and amino acids where you store the pent-up emotions, finally being able to release, let go, and forgive.

When you forgive, you are forgiving the past and letting go of the effects a situation has on you. You are not condoning, making light of, or denying the seriousness of what may happened. You are simply giving yourself permission to bring more peace and freedom into your life.

Being able to forgive can empower you to recognise the pain you suffered without letting that pain define you, enabling you to heal and move on with your life. This reminds us of another quote we are fond of: "When you choose to forgive those who have hurt you, you take away their power and regain it for yourself."

36. Be in the Now

What are you aware of right now? We invite you to stop reading and notice this.

Are you aware of what happened before you began reading this? Or perhaps you are aware of what you are going to do later? Whatever you are aware of, we are sure it is more than just this moment, your now. And, in a way that is unfortunate because you are missing a small part of your now—a moment in time you will never get back.

Now, if you are just sitting here reading this, that might not matter so much. But, when you are with a friend or loved one, you may be missing out on precious time while being consumed or distracted by things that don't belong in your now.

NLP will help you to become more aware of your moments and more able to be in the now. You will learn a process called **clearing your now**, created by Dr Heidi. The purpose of **clearing your now** is specifically to help you be more present. You'll also be able to create an anchor, which is a stimulus that can help trigger your state of being present. Additionally, if you have a pattern of worrying, fidgeting, being distracted, overwhelmed, or focused on things other than the present, you will gain skills about how to change those unuseful patterns.

You see, some people don't *want* to live more in the now because they have unconscious programming that requires certainty, and the now can be sometimes uncertain as you don't know what is coming up next. So, living in the past or future becomes easier. Of course, you can't continually live in the now; how would you plan for the future or learn from the past? But you should be able to spend a good amount of time in your now. So, if there are patterns or programs that stop you from doing so, you can alter them with NLP.

Perhaps you are already aware of the great benefits of being in the now? To name just a few, as an enticement to live more in the present: being in the now will help you to have more energy, more time, and be more engaged in relationships; you will be able to manage pain more effectively; choose what you eat, fully enjoy food, and eat less of it! Being more in the now will help you to be more creative, less judgemental, and will also help you to identify what is really going on with you.

Imagine, being able fully experience life more, in ways that can allow you more pleasure—in the now.

37. Become More Mindful

For the past few years, the concept of **mindfulness** has become all the rage. When we talk about being mindful, initial thoughts of it include meditation, finding a Zen-like state, and yogic breathing. And yes, that is one type of mindfulness, but what NLP can help you achieve is mindfulness during your daily life.

Ultimately, being mindful simply means *being aware*. Aware of yourself, the impact you are making in the moment, and aware of others around you.

In daily life, meditating may not help you be more aware in the moment, but it might help you keep your cool throughout the day! What will help is to expand your own awareness about yourself and others around you. With NLP, you will learn to develop your **sensory acuity** awareness; that is, increase your awareness of your heightened senses of what is happening in the moment, for you and the people around you.

Being more mindful has been correlated to a greater sense of well-being, happiness, and health. When you are more present and mindful in the moment worry, anxiety, depression, and illness can diminish, leaving you in the moment with more awareness of right here and right now.

Not only will NLP share sensory acuity skills, but you will also be able to anchor mindfulness into your day. Perhaps you might set an alarm, or use your phone ring as an anchor, or the cry of a child as a reminder to stop for a moment and be aware; tune into the moment and the world around you and simply be aware.

When you can create a habit of mindfulness, unresourceful emotions and behaviours have a harder time of penetrating your now. You will be more aware of your interactions in the world and more choices will become available to you.

When we let our mind run amok, it will think that it is in charge of us. However, with simple techniques and skills, you can harness your conscious thinking mind and take back your choice, power, and mindfulness, one moment at a time.

38. Enhance Your Creativity

Your beautiful unconscious mind is a very creative being indeed. When we start to talk to people about being creative, we are often told, "Oh, no! I'm not creative. I can't draw or anything." Being creative doesn't have anything to do with artistic abilities; it is about being able to see outside the square, read between the lines, solve problems, know which shoes go with your outfit, and how to be flexible in different situations.

Innately, everyone is creative; how much creativity you display to the world depends greatly on your beliefs and values. If it is important to get things right, be perfect, and have answers, you are less likely to be as creative as you might be. If you fear failure, dislike criticism, or if you need the approval of others, again, you may lack some creative flair.

However, creativity lives within you. Look at children for this; most kids can imagine and be creative without the fears or limitations holding them back and getting in their way. At some point, however, we develop inhibitions and start to care what others think; we start to care if we're doing something right and our creative juices start to dry up.

Does it have to be that way? Nope, not at all!

With NLP, you can change beliefs, realign values, and step back into your creative self, without limits and without hesitation. In fact, if you don't believe that you have ever been creative, you can use NLP to model someone else who is creative, and create that for yourself.

At the end of the day, you are in charge of your mind. You might as well be in charge of your creativity too!

39. Be Less Serious and Having More Fun

When you watch a child, you can see a freedom, a curiosity, and a willingness to play. Wouldn't it be wonderful to have more of that as an adult?

When did growing up mean being more serious and having less fun? I mean, how dull is that! Where in the world did all this serious business come from?

The serious answer, is it came from our programming when we were younger. As a kid, you were allowed the freedom to be a kid. *That* was your job. But somewhere along the line, you learned that as you grow up, you aren't allowed the same level of freedom. Until you are around the age of 13, you are modelling the people around you. By this age, you know the rules of being a serious adult. You have beliefs about being responsible, serious, and trustworthy. You know the rules about having fun, messing around, and playing.

But is it really supposed to be so serious? We don't think so. Neither did Oscar Wilde; he is quoted to have said, "Life is too important to be taken seriously." How true is that!

Here's the good news. You *know* how to be less serious and more fun! You may not have given yourself permission to let your hair down for a long time, but you know how. Your cells contain the memories of you being a kid. Even if you had to grow up too fast, like many kids did, you still had moments as a child, toddler, or baby where you were free to play and be.

With NLP, you will gain insight into how to reboot your mind and body back to times when you had permission to play and you can again capture more of those moments of freedom, being care-free, and having fun.

Imagine the ability to have more fun and be less serious in life. Do you think you could bring in fun to situations that aren't necessarily fun? That meeting you're about to go to, that challenging conversation, parenting?

There are so many moments in life that would benefit from bringing in the lightness and joy that can come from having more fun and being less serious!

40. Identify Your Values

Do you know what is important to you? When we ask this question in NLP, we are asking you about your values.

Values are what is important to you and can be driving factors, which can provide continual motivation and drive to be the best you can be.

We have values for absolutely everything in life: how you learn, what you learn, relationships, how you communicate, finance and money—everything! When your values are being met, you can find yourself in a state of flow, congruence, and alignment in that area of life. When your values are not being met, there is usually a sense of disease, discomfort, incongruence, and feeling like something isn't quite right.

Values are a very important aspect to success and well-being. These can be simple concepts like being organised, growth, or certainty, and they can also be more abstract concepts such as freedom, peace, or wholeness.

With NLP, not only will you be able to identify your values in different aspects of life, but you will also learn strategies to ensure your values are being met, tools to change beliefs and even processes to update any values which may be outdated or redundant.

41. Create More External Awareness

We're sure you have met those people who are so very unaware of what is going on outside of their heads. You might be talking to one of them and they don't observe the subtle cues you give them that its time to go, or you've heard that story before, or you understand their message. They keep talking and walking with you, and they keep on keeping on. This same person might step out in front of you when you're walking and be completely oblivious to your existence. Or step into the shopping queue before you and a bunch of others because they didn't even notice a line there.

In NLP, we deem this as having a lack of **sensory acuity**. Sensory acuity is a tool that you will learn in NLP which will help you to be more aware of the macro and micro aspects of the world around you. You'll be able to identify when someone understands you (or if they don't), when someone is ready to go, when they want to engage, and when their emotions or energy has shifted.

You will learn an aspect of peripheral vision which will help you to be more aware of others and their place in your world. This means no more running into people, cutting people off, and not listening! Sensory acuity skills are amazing to improve your communication skills and general understanding of others and the world around you.

42. Create More Internal Awareness

Sensory acuity is a great skill to have with others and the world around you, it is also an exceptional tool to have for yourself. Too many people don't put their own needs first and they don't recognise when their mind/body is communicating with them.

With NLP and sensory acuity skills, you will also learn to tune more into yourself. You'll be able to listen and trust your unconscious mind more, notice more of your intuition, be clearer in your mind, and more determined in your way of being.

What we've found is when our students start to apply their sensory acuity skills to themselves, they begin to better **respect their own model of the world** and start to give them what they need. Imagine really being able to understand what you need from yourself!

And guess what, those little aches and pains, or a headache, or hunger when you're stressed, or the need for a cigarette, or depression or anxiety? All of that is your body's way to communicate with you. Won't it be great to have the tools available to truly can listen to yourself in a new and more powerful way?

43. Leave a Legacy

Do you want to leave a legacy? Or maybe they don't remember you specifically, but something you did or created or encouraged in others?

Recently I was having a conversation about NLP helping someone to leave a legacy and was asked quite incredulously, "How can NLP help me leave a legacy? Like I do a process and people remember me?"

Well, no.

NLP will help you to leave a legacy, because NLP is more than just a set of tools. It is an attitude.

Richard Bandler, one of the founders of NLP, often said that, "**NLP is an attitude of curiosity and a methodology which leave a trail of techniques**." This attitude of curiosity is an interesting one. Most exceptional NLPers that we know have this attitude of curiosity about themselves, their life, and about growth and personal transformation.

With NLP, you do not have a magic key to success; you have many keys to unlocking potentials within yourself and others. You will be able to better understand yourself so that you can live as authentically and as congruently as possible. People remember that!

You will learn how to identify your motivational triggers to use them more, how to create anchors to get yourself into peak states of performance (or disconnection if you desire down-time), how to identify and change behaviours, beliefs, thoughts, attitudes, and concepts, how to align your intentions and behaviours, how to understand and use the unconscious patterns of others, how to use your mindset to set and achieve goals, and ultimately how to get the most out of your life experience.

If you can live your best life, be an exemplar for doing so and let other people see your light shine, you will leave a legacy. In fact, you'll leave a living legacy throughout your life, too.

44. Get Your Psychology Right for Relationships

Where did you learn to 'do' relationships? Most likely, from your parents, who learned from their parents, who learned from their parents, who learned from their parents; and so on. And, if your family history is like 90% of the population, there was probably some sort of dysfunction going on that you learned, modelled, fought from, absorbed, or rebelled against.

Most often, our current and present state is a culmination of what we have learned in the past, and we learn a lot when we are young by modelling, observing, and absorbing rules, norms, behaviours, attitudes, and beliefs. When a coaching client comes to see us about improving their skills in relationships, one of the first questions we ask is, "Where did you learn to 'do' relationships?"

All the patterns that we did model and learn while growing up, and even as young adults and adults about relationships are unconscious patterns of behaviour, emotion, and belief. Because of this, we can apply a variety of NLP tools to create more effective patterns.

NLP will help you to address beliefs that may not be serving you now. For example, if a child modelled a jealous or mistrusting parent then there is more likelihood that as an adult these same behaviours will be exhibited—even without reason for them. If a child experienced abandonment from loved ones, there is a good chance they will protect against being abandoned as an adult in relationships.

We meet many people who have created dependency patterns, or addiction to love patterns which mean they continually need to be in a relationship to feel whole. NLP is based on an aspect that people work best when they themselves are whole and integrated with themselves. So, NLP will help you to not just set up success for relationships with others, but to help you create a dynamic relationship with yourself, setting your psychology right from the beginning.

45. Improve Your Relationship with Money

How's your money situation? Do you have a good relationship with it? Do you have enough of it? Or is there not enough month at the end of your money?

Have you ever thought that your bank balance could be a direct result of your psychological and unconscious relationship with money?

We've found that often, when people have a lack of money they also *have* beliefs that are not aligned with having an abundance of it. We hear a lot of beliefs like, "money is evil," "having money means I'm greedy," "only pretentious people have money," "money can't buy you happiness," and so many other clichés that we're sure you've heard, too.

But what if it is those very clichés that are holding you back from having what you want in terms of finances and money?

Your unconscious mind is responsible for eavesdropping on your thoughts and what is being done or said around you. In the formative years, from birth until around age 7, you are a sponge just soaking up information. Very few filters are in place and your mind is creating beliefs that will shape your future. With NLP, you can reshape it.

For example, we recently worked with a young man in his mid-twenties with NLP and his relationship with money. We used a few NLP tools, but the most beneficial was accessing his timeline to identify *when* his patterns began with money. Most people do not consciously remember much from their past, but your unconscious mind stores everything. Sometimes memories are presented to us in the form of a movie, which may or may not be *true*, but the mind is very metaphorical, so whatever comes up, we trust that will give us the learnings or understandings we need.

This young man created a movie of a boy that was about 2 years old. The boy had been given a few dollars to spend in the shop and he promptly spent it all on some candy. From somewhere in the movie, someone said, "He can't even hang on to a few bucks! He spends it like there is no tomorrow."

Again, the unconscious mind is continually eavesdropping on, and taking personally and literally, everything that is happening around us. When someone of importance speaks about us or to us when we are in these formative years, beliefs can be created. And one was made for this man; a belief that he can't hang onto money. And, he couldn't. As soon as he got some money, he would spend it. He lived this belief as if it were his truth. Because for him, it was!

We changed this belief using NLP and from there, his behaviours began to change too. He could even *save* money!

Regardless of what your beliefs are or how your current behaviours are displayed in your life, you can change anything that isn't working for you or servicing your desires. With NLP, you can create a dynamic and beneficial relationship with money that will meet and exceed your personal and professional goals.

46. Improve Your Relationship with Time

Strange question, but what is your relationship with time like?

Some people have a hard time with time; being late, rushed, waiting until a deadline, getting anxious, creating stress, getting lost in time. Other people are good friends with time. They manage time well, prioritise, get things done, are early, know how much time is left, and plan well.

We all know that time doesn't actually exist. Well, sure, the sun goes around the earth every 24 hours, but the concept of time is a man-made aspect. Your mind and body don't know or understand time. If there was any sense of time, your mind and body would be 'now.'

Think about a baby for a moment. It needs to be trained to sleep through the night and to eat at certain times. Until that training occurs, it sleeps and eats whenever it wants and whenever it can. At some point in the first few years of life we start to learn and understand the concept of time.

In fact, once you learn time, did you know that your mind created a specific code so that it could tell the difference between the past, present, and future? Otherwise, it would all be jumbled up. Your mind has this coding for everything; every belief, concept, idea, memory, and every-thing.

Have you ever seen someone say, "I'll get to that later," and they use their hand to motion to the left or in front of them? Or, "Oh, that's behind me," meaning the past? This is a tiny insight into how a person codes their **timeline**. Just like history has a timeline, so do you; it is your mind's coding to separate the past, present, and future so you know if something is already complete or if it is yet to come.

In NLP, we call this coding **Submodalities;** these are the building blocks or coding of our mind. Our Submodalities are the sub-components of our 5 senses. These micro details of our thoughts have memories coded in certain ways; some memories are in colour while some are in black-and-white. Sometime we see or feel an image in our mind that is big and others are small. When talking about the Submodalities of time, time is generally coded in location, direction, distance, and size.

For example, a person may store or code their **past** about 2 feet to the left, their **now** directly in front of them and their **future** another 2 feet to their right. Another person may store their past behind them, their now inside of them and their future in front of them.

The mind is very metaphorical and can tell us a little about the relationship people have with time. If someone's past is too close to them (distance), often they feel pressured by the past. Similarly, if a someone's future is too close, they may feel pressured by the future. If the size of a person's now (energetically speaking) is small, there might be a sense of overwhelm, and too big the person may be bored. We've also found that if a person's future is higher than eye level (location) they can relate to things like, "My goals are just outside of my grasp," "It's like an uphill climb to get what I want," and "I feel like I take 2 steps forward and one step back,"

Through various studies, NLP researchers have found that if a person stores their entire timeline outside of their body, they will naturally be good at time management, organising time, being on time, and completing tasks. In fact, if your timeline is all outside of your body, you probably tend to take time personally. That is, if someone is late for a meeting or appointment with you, you take it personally.

Conversely, this same NLP research has found that if any of your timeline passes inside of your body, then you may get lost in time, manage time ineffectively, and be prone to being late, procrastination, and doing things at the last minute.

When you learn NLP, you will not only learn about your specific coding or how you store time, you'll also be able to alter and change it as you desire. If time used to be a pressure point and that isn't useful, you can change it. If you want more time in the now, you can create it. If you want time to move quicker, you can change the size of how your now is stored. Amazingly and easily, when you learn NLP you will create a better, more fluid relationship with time.

47. Improve Your Relationship with Food

Do you love food? Like really love it and crave it? Or maybe you just like it. Or, maybe you see food as just sustenance and fuel for the body.

Whatever your mindset, emotional ties and beliefs are about food; they are the basis of your relationship with food. At the end of the day, food is just sustenance and fuel for the body, but we humans often put more meaning on it that just fuel. We get emotional about food. I'm not sure it's just a human thing! I've seen how crazy my pets get over cheese! But, I've never seen a dog comfort eat or do mindless snacking when they are bored. Those traits are exclusive to humans.

NLP will assist you to revaluate your relationship with food, the meanings you put on food, the beliefs you hold, and the behaviours you have with food.

I'm sure you've heard of people who stress eat, or get *hangry* (angry when they are hungry), or eat when they are bored, or stop eating when they are stressed, or binge when they have a problem, or starve when they are lacking emotional connection, or eat when they are lonely.

None of that is about food. All of it is about you. And, you are in charge of your mind and emotions; therefore, you are also in charge of your relationship with food.

Recently, we met a woman who wanted help with NLP to stop eating candy and sweets; she blamed her behaviour on stress. After some investigation and communicating with her craving for sweets, she identified that the sweets were keeping her busy and keeping her thoughts away from the unhappiness she felt in her marriage. It had nothing to do with the sugary delights at all.

You will be learning how to communicate with your mind/body connection, identify and clear beliefs that are not serving you, change behaviours to more empowering ones, and improve your personal relationship with food.

Of course, you can still appreciate, love, desire, and crave food; there isn't anything wrong with that, as long as the relationship with food is one that is not dependant on food to be anything other than good tasting, and sometimes good for you!

48. Improve Your Relationship with Energy

Do you ever feel listless, tired, drained, or lacking in energy? Do you have strategies to help you with it so that you can bounce of bed and get on with your day in the way you want to? Okay, so you might not want to *bounce* out of bed! But what do you do on days where you are lacking energy?

Sometimes we don't have energy because we haven't gotten enough rest or we're not fuelling our body with the right nutrients. Sometimes low energy is a result of too much brain power being expanded, stress, depression, or overwhelm pulling resources from our energy reserves. So, what can you about this?

From NLP, we learn that you have all the resources you need to achieve your desired state. Resources here include any attitudes, attributes, skills, or emotions, including energy. What we've often found is that when someone has low energy, they don't have a clear desired state or direction. Motivation, drive, and energy boosts are created when we are moving in a clear direction with focus and attention on the desired result.

In times when you have no aim, direction or focus that you are more likely to lack energy.

Think about the first few days of a vacation, when you finally stop *doing* and start doing nothing. Chances are, your energy will dip and you'll find yourself tired and exhausted. The mind and body aren't used to doing nothing. In times like these, our body creates and secretes less of the chemicals needed to boost your mood, emotion, and energy. For a day or so at the beginning of a vacation, this tired feeling may be useful to reboot your system and get you ready to *do* your vacation. However, imagine if that was your life. Doing nothing, feeling nothing, and having no energy to do anything anyway. This is what depression is.

If you don't have energy at various times then NLP will help you to align with a desired state; you'll learn how to create a **well-formed outcome**, which is a goal with emotional attachment and steps to achieve it; you'll be able to create a **resource anchor** that helps you to step into a state of energy, power and motivation; and you'll be able to be more mindful and aware of the states you are in at any given time.

If your lack of energy is more chronic—if it's been around for a while and is tied to other things like depression, illness, anxiety, stress, worry, or over-thinking—then NLP can be helpful in other ways too. You will learn skills to change patterns of emotions, beliefs, and behaviours so you can address the root cause of any energy leaks. You will learn how to model yourself and others to change your behaviours and unconscious programming to attract, keep, and use the energy levels you desire to have.

When you can improve your relationship with energy, you will feel better, sleep better, you'll be more creative, you'll think more clearly, and you'll ultimately live a better life. If you currently don't have a great relationship with your energy, what is stopping you from making a change now?

49. Improve Your Relationship with Yourself

NLP often looks at the presence of rapport with someone to identify where a conflict or miscommunication comes from. Rapport is that connection that you have with someone that often makes it safe, easy, and supportive to be with someone. There is an assumption about communication from NLP that says, "Resistance is a sign of a lack of rapport."

Most often, this assumption is gathered about rapport with other people, but what about rapport with yourself? For us to be truly content, congruent and happy, the relationship we cultivate with ourselves may just be the most important one in life.

While NLP has a focus on communication and modelling excellence in interpersonal relationships), it equally has a quieter objective to assist you in developing an exceptional intrapersonal relationship with yourself.

When you learn NLP, you will not only be learning how to understand others, you'll be starting with yourself as a guide. Modelling excellence from the inside out, if you will.

The relationship you have with yourself is largely based on your personal **model of the world**, which is made up of your entire history, beliefs, behaviours, attitudes, emotions, memories, patterns, and resources. Each of us has a different tapestry that makes us who we are.

Sometimes, the unconscious elements of us like our beliefs, attitudes, emotions, and self-concepts are either not aligned to who we want to be or who we think we *should* be. Through self-evaluation and introspection, using some of the tools of NLP, you will not only be able to better understand your own model of the world, you will also be able to clear any interferences, beliefs, blocks, or barriers to truly being you. Even if that first means figuring out who you are.

You will be delving into your values, ideals, goals, beliefs, unconscious patterns, and so much more. By uncovering **who** you truly are, you will be able to better respect your own model of the world, get closer to who you want to be, and ultimately, improve the most important relationship in your life.

50. Create More Certainty in Your Life

Tony Robbins is known to declare that to be happy we need to have both certainty and uncertainty in our lives. However, many people find certainty boring or too rigid or too familiar. Often, we see these people and call them 'risk takers' or 'adrenaline junkies' or 'drama queens,' creating uncertainty when certainty could easily exist.

What is it that makes one person crave the unknown and uncertainty and others are drawn more to what they can count on? The simple answer is beliefs.

If a person believes that change is the only certainty, they are going to be more familiar and possibly more comfortable with uncertainty. This in turn can lead to things in life like an inability to be stable in relationships, jobs, living situations, and more. It creates a driver for change, which, isn't necessarily useful for creating long-term stability.

With NLP, you can create more certainty in your life by addressing any patterns of beliefs and emotions which may not align with certainty and developing a desire for more stability and security. This might mean taking out the 'boring' beliefs and increasing desire for sameness.

Now, this doesn't mean creating a total life of certainty; remember, we need a balance of certainty and uncertainty in our lives.

51. Become Okay with Uncertainty

We need a balance of certainty and uncertainty in our lives. Too much of either, and life gets either boring or hectic. But, some people do not like uncertainty and do whatever they can to create more certainty around them.

Uncertainty is the unknowingness of what is about to happen. It is often where the good stuff in life comes from! And, it is all around. I don't know what the weather will be like tomorrow (the weather app is often changing its mind!), I don't know how a book or movie ends, if a relationship is going to work out or not, how someone will respond to a question I ask, what the traffic is going to be like on my way to work, and many, many other things.

There are so many things in our lives that are uncertain; it is nearly imperative that a person is okay with the unknown.

Needing certainty in life can create a lot of issues like anxiety, depression, procrastination, perfectionism, or the tried and true paralysis-by-analysis. The very aspect of trying to create certainty out of uncertainty is quite stressful and provokes and creates more cortisol and adrenaline to be released into the bloodstream.

When you learn NLP, you can help yourself become more okay with uncertainty by addressing any of the underlying beliefs, thoughts, and behaviours around this pattern. For example, many people lack a sense of security of safety and feel the need to surround themselves with certainty. Others have a fear of failure, and won't start anything until they know for certain that something will work (this often leads to procrastination, because really, can one ever be absolutely certain about anything?).

In NLP, you will learn techniques that help you to access your warehouse of memories so that you can find where the unconscious patterns began in your life so that you will be able to review those events from a more mature and dissociated manner. This in turn will allow you to re-evaluate your past experiences and make new choices for now based on what your desires and intentions are currently.

A presupposition from NLP is that **all NLP should increase choice and wholeness,** and in doing so, this will help you create more congruence with uncertainty, and then create a balance between the known and the unknown in your life, which, in turn can develop into a growth mindset versus a fixed mindset that often accompanies not accessing uncertainty.

52. Work with the Law of Attraction

There is a saying: "Energy goes where your attention flows," and that is, where we put our focus is what we bring into our lives, or the Law of Attraction.

Ultimately, the law of attraction says that we can influence our lives by directing our thoughts to what we want instead of what we don't want. NLP takes this concept a few steps further with more understanding of how the unconscious mind works and how we can sabotage those efforts by outdated programming.

Let's first explore the unconscious mind. Your unconscious mind is said to make up 90% of the conscious/unconscious mind. The 10% of your conscious mind is responsible for thinking, analysing, and reasoning. The remainder is your unconscious mind and it is responsible for everything else: the running of your body, processing of emotions, storing all your memories, triggering all the programs of emotion, behaviour, belief, and thought that you have.

Much like a computer, the unconscious mind simply processes information about what is going on around us and in us. It doesn't judge, translate, or decipher. It just takes in and gives out information as it was programmed to do. Largely, our programming is based on our history and is made up of the beliefs, filters, triggers, emotions, and memories of both the remembered and forgotten.

When talking about the law of attraction, the unconscious mind has a few key roles to play, in addition to simply processing information. It takes everything personally and literally and is unable to judge. This means, that what you say to yourself or what other people say about you, your mind will take personally. If your internal dialogue is filled with positive, powerful, and purposeful statements, it will run that as the sound track of your life and colour your world with this view. If, on the other hand, the sound track you play is of fear, failure or worries, this, too, will cloud your view.

But, it's not just as simple as changing your language. Sure, that is a great first step, and I'm sure you've heard **change your thinking, change your life**, and to a great extent that is true, but its missing something. Sometimes the patterns that we run create sabotaging effects on our desires.

For example, a person may have a fear of being abandoned or left behind; that fear may trump any affirmation or positive thinking about finding a long term committed relationship because it conflicts with it.

A person who desires starting their own business and working independently may not succeed because they have a need for security and certainty that doesn't always align with entrepreneurship.

Another person may be using the law of attraction to lose weight, get in shape, and feel better, but if they have a pattern of not wanting to be noticed, or a belief that losing weight is hard, they will find it challenging to lose weight.

So, with NLP, you will not only look at your desired state through a lens of the law of attraction, you will also identify any possible barriers to your success and can remove those barriers with a variety of techniques from NLP.

What we think truly does affect what we believe and what we do; what we belief affects what we do and what we think; and what we do affects what we think about what we believe. NLP will help you finally align what you think, believe and do so you can truly work with the law of attraction.

53. Develop More Emotional Intelligence

Have you ever watched *The Big Bang Theory*? If so, you will know of the character Sheldon Cooper who has little ability to identify the emotions of others; he is often blunt, disrespectful and clueless when it comes to his responses and interactions. Sheldon has a very high **intelligence quotient (IQ)** and a very low **emotional intelligence quotient (EQ)**.

In 1983, psychologist Howard Gardener introduced his concept of **multiple intelligences**. Two of the intelligent he included were both **interpersonal intelligence** (the ability to understand the emotions, motivations and desires of others), and **intrapersonal intelligence** (the ability to understand the emotions, feelings, and motivations of yourself). This was the basis of **Emotional Intelligence**.

Emotional intelligence can be defined as the ability to recognise emotions of self and others, discern between different feelings, and use this information as a guide to thinking and communicating while managing their emotions and responses appropriately. Studies have shown that people with higher EQ have greater job performance, leadership skills, mental health, and relationship success.

Because a focus of NLP is on respecting and staying flexible to the different models of the world around you, NLP will offer you a variety of tools and concepts that will keep you in a growth mindset and expand on your own emotional intelligence.

With NLP, you will learn how to have more sensory acuity, which is the skill often lacking when someone has low emotional intelligent. It is the ability to be more aware to the sensory elements around you, primarily what you see and what you hear. Changes in tonality, tempo volume, facial expressions, body posture, breathing, and blinking all have unconscious meaning behind them. When you can be more aware to the non-verbal communication from another person, you can then begin to calibrate for meaning, which is the use of your emotional intelligence.

Additionally, NLP will unpack and teach you how to build rapport with anyone quickly and efficiently. Rapport is the ability to open a connection between yourself and others where communication and energy can easily flow. Rapport will help you to be able to tune in and connect with others. You'll also learn how to use various perceptual positions of others so you could metaphorically step into the shoes of someone else and tap into their unconscious mind, emotions, feelings, behaviours, and thoughts. To do so creates an intimate connection of understanding and emotional flow.

Finally, if you have any block, barriers, or reservations about increasing your emotional awareness of yourself and others, NLP can help you to identify and clear those blocks. By changing a belief or concept around emotional intelligence, you are already opening the pathway to more understanding and bonding with others in a meaningful way.

More and more we are seeing the increase of evaluating and developing their staffs' emotional intelligence in job performance, and companies are more likely to hire people who already great interpersonal communication skills. The development of emotional intelligence with NLP will provide you with more personal competence and understanding others and effectively navigating the relationships in your life.

54. Take Responsibility for Your Life

Recently I was at a restaurant on my own, and before I picked up my book to be absorbed in another world, I began to eavesdrop on the people next to me. One was complaining about how hard it was to lose weight (while adding copious amounts of sugar to her coffee, eating sweet breads and fried food), another person was complaining about a work colleague and how little he felt understood and the third person was talking about a shoulder pain she had been having for a few years (she even remarked at how easy it is to make pain feel *normal*).

Now, I have no real judgement about any of these people, but I do have an observation: none are fully taking responsibility for what is going on in their lives.

I'd like to point out or remind you about 3 presuppositions or assumptions that the filter of NLP has: 1) you are in charge of your mind and therefore your results, 2) your mind and body are connected and therefore affect each other, and 3) the person with the most flexibility will control their situation.

When you learn NLP, and embody the elements that fit for you, one thing you will notice is an elevated sense of responsibility in your life. In *your life*. You will also begin to be even more aware of the role others have for their own life. It still amazes me, all these years after first learning NLP how little responsibility some people take for their lives.

If I had permission to discuss NLP and personal responsibility and choice to the table next to me at the restaurant I would share with them some of the ways they can help themselves and take back ownership of their destiny.

I would say to the woman who wants to lose weight that sugar didn't just jump in your coffee and those pastries didn't magically appear on your plate. You have choice here. You are the only one responsible for what you are doing right here in this moment. If you don't have a clear desired state or plan of action, NLP can help you create this. If there are cravings that you can't control about what you're eating, NLP can help you change or manage those too. But, at the end of the day, it is up to you.

To the gentleman who didn't feel understood, I would ask him how he would know if others did understand him. I'd inquire about who he feels misunderstood by and explain that if there is a pattern in his life of feeling this way, NLP can help him to change that pattern and possibly even understand himself better. I'd explain that NLP could help him to express himself more effectively, enhance his confidence and personal power if needed, and give himself permission to be understood. I'd also share with him that if he first sought to understand others, then perhaps he could more clearly help people to also understand him. I would help him understand that it is his responsibility for people to understand him, not the other way around.

To the lady with shoulder pain, I'd first let her know that it *isn't* normal and that if she chooses to she doesn't have to live with it. I'd explain the mind/body connection and let her know that her pain probably has less to do with her posture and more to do with an emotion or belief she is holding onto. I'd also tell her that she is in charge of her mind and her body and she could use her mind to understand and get rid of her pain; she could be empowered to know what her body is communicating to her so that in the future, should she feel this pain again and she would know what to do.

When teaching and sharing NLP with our students, it is important for us to empower them to take responsibility for what is going on in life. Take responsibility for everything that is going right, so you can do that over and over again. Take responsibility for what isn't going well, so you can change it.

55. Get Clear About What Matters to You

When was the last time you took a close look at what matters to you? If you are like most people, you have never spent quality time on this task; you probably just take what matters to you for granted. And, ultimately, that is okay, unless you want to create something different in your life. You see, if you *want* something different, you must *do* something different.

When we start to talk from an NLP perspective about what matters to you, the question we're really asking is, "What do you value and believe?" or, "What is important to you and why?"

When you can get clear about what matters to you—in all aspects of life (work, hope, relationships, money, health, etc.)—then you can be more mindful, purposeful, and proactive to create more happiness and success in your life. One aim of NLP is to create more personal wholeness and choice in life. By knowing what matters to you, you can access more wholeness, congruence, and more alignment in your day to day life.

With NLP, you will be introduced to the motivational traits that your beliefs and values have. You will investigate into your own life to identify what is important to you, what values you hold true, what ideals you wish to uphold, and what beliefs hold them in place or what beliefs undermine your values.

Empowered with this information, you will be able to be your own coach in life. As your own coach, you can create a roadmap to success, identify what resources you need to access and build, and learn what conscious or unconscious patterns or programs may be holding you back.

At its core, NLP is more than just an investigation tool. It also provides you skills and resources to get closer to what matters to you so that you can be more aligned, authentic and living on purpose. All of that can start with getting clear about what matters to you in the first place.

56. Find Your Authentic Self

Do you know anyone who walks around the world with different masks? Like they have to be different people for different people? That would be a hard way to live; it would take a lot of emotional and physical energy to do!

NLP will help you to find your true, authentic self, and even give yourself permission to live in a congruent and authentic way. You will learn about your programs, filters, beliefs. and values, which are the driving forces of who you are. And, you'll learn how to change what isn't working and to align what is so that you are more free to just be yourself.

Too many times masks come up when a person doesn't feel safe or comfortable in a situation, and we think this is very normal. But, what happens if a person doesn't feel safe or comfortable in general? We have met a lot of people, students and clients, who tell us things like, "I think people will eventually notice that I'm a fraud," (in my job, relationship, life, etc.), because not being authentic is hard.

With your NLP skills, you'll be building more self-confidence, tapping into your self-worth and removing the layers of protection, barriers, and boundaries that may have been put up over the years. One of the absolute best things for us as NLP Trainers, we get to watch those layers come off and a beautiful you emerge from within!

57. Create a Stream of Abundance

When you think of abundance, what do you think of? Most people think of money. Having a stream of money would be amazing, wouldn't it? Of course, abundance can come in any form of energy: time, money, health, physical energy, love, prosperity, friendship

From an NLP perspective, if you have any current (or old!) beliefs, behaviours, ideas, or concepts of your identity that block you from creating abundance, you can address them. You will be able to change unresourceful beliefs, create new behaviours that are more aligned with what you want, realign your thinking to draw toward you more of what you want, and you'll even be able to address *who* you are and make sure the identity you portray to the world is also in alignment with what you desire to bring into your life.

If you have beliefs or ideas that something is hard, or takes hard work, or should be challenging to be rewarding, a stream of abundance would look more like white-water rapids! The unconscious mind works with the Law of Attraction—where your attention goes your energy flows—so, you might as well use NLP to help you align yourself with an abundance of everything you want!

58. Create a Growth vs. Fixed Mindset

Two of the premise NLP is based on is **choice is better than no choice**, and **NLP should create choice and wholeness**. Therefore, when we are looking at the aspect of a growth versus fixed mindset, NLP is focused on growth.

Something you will learn again and again is that the person who has the most flexibility in behaviour will more easily control the situation. If you are selling a product or service and you have it in your mind that you must do it in a certain way, then you potentially could be missing out on sales. If you want to motivate your child but only have one strategy, you may not be very successful. If you are trying to solve a problem and only have one idea, what happens if it doesn't work?

We meet people a lot who are fixed in their mind-set. They have learned that knowing, having certainty and doing something in a ridged manner will get them their outcome. And, sometimes they are correct. But, what has found in various studies, is that when people can adapt, be flexible and grow, they are more likely to be successful, happy, and balanced.

While some people do tend to have more of a fixed mindset, this isn't a hardwired program; it is learned and can be changed. We've found that the fixed mindset comes in when people don't like change, have a fear of failure, a dislike of the unknown, desire certainty, are past-focused, or are unable to associate to a different future. With NLP tools that deal with changing unconscious programs of behaviour, thought, and emotion we can crack the surface of a fixed mindset.

Once cracked, we can make way for a new mindset based on growth, change, and flexibility. Sometimes this is easier said than done. Most adults don't take well to criticism, feedback, and being challenged. Often, in these types of situations we revert to a *fixed-mindset*, mainly due to ego and fear of not being good enough. If this comes up as a pattern or belief, NLP can help you to address and change this unconscious programming. You may also benefit from using NLP to help you to build and access resilience, self-esteem, and self-worth for times when a fixed-mindset comes out to play.

We don't profess that a person could or even should have a growth-mindset all the time. What we do know however, is that with more openness to growing, your life will be richer, more expansive, and you'll be more balanced and complete.

59. Manage Your Internal Dialogue

There is a great quote that says, "The most important words you will ever utter are those you say to yourself, about yourself, when you are by yourself." This is such a powerful statement; our internal dialogue is a guide for our lives, and you cannot turn it off. What you can do however is manage your thoughts, your mind, and your internal dialogue.

It is your thoughts that often drive your motivation, determination, choices, and life. And our thoughts have a great deal of power over us. Henry Ford had it right when he said, "If you think you can or think you cannot, you are correct." But where does your internal dialogue come from?

Your internal dialogue comes from a culmination of your model of the world; all the experiences you had, the memories you've got, the emotions you've lived, the beliefs you have, the behaviours you do—all of this makes up your model of the world.

It is the outcome of your life that creates your thoughts. Additionally, it is the quality of your thoughts that creates your life. Can you feel this dance in action?

What you think affects what you feel, which effects what you do. What you feel affects what you do and what you think. What you think affects what you feel and what you do.

A circle. Sometimes a vicious circle, depending on the quality of your thoughts.

So, if our thoughts are so important and we can't stop the internal dialogue, I have a question for you. How do you know to believe your internal dialogue or not? If it says you are stupid or if it says you are brilliant. How do you know to believe it?

Ultimately, that will come down to the feeling it gives and the unconscious programs the internal dialogue connects to. You see, this is the finest element of NLP in action. Unconsciously, your mind is paying attention to what is being said, done, seen, thought, felt (the linguistic of NLP), and this automatically taps into our neurology; a chemical or hormone is secreted (neuro) and this automatically triggers a response (programming). Whatever the response is, this is the programming. If your mind says, 'you are stupid,' and your response is an affirming one with defeating emotions, unresourceful beliefs, and low self- worth, you will take this statement as true and continue to respond accordingly.

Using this understanding of how the language of our mind creates and taps into our unconscious programming, we can do something about it. With your NLP skills, you will be able to identify and change beliefs, decisions, and emotions that are triggered from your internal dialogue. This in turn changes you feel, thus also changing your internal dialogue and behaviours. Again, the circle. But, this time a circle of thoughts, feeling, and action that you manage.

Undoubtedly, thought this book you've read the NLP assumption you are in charge of your mind and therefore your results countless times. When you can truly manage your internal dialogue, you will be in charge of your mind, and from there, the rest of your life too. Remember: you don't want to stop your internal dialogue, you want to manage it so that it doesn't manage you.

NLP for Exceptional Communication

"We all communicate, all the time. With NLP, you will not only become a better communicator, you will create elegance with listening, understanding, asking questions and being curious about yourself and other people. That – is the makings of an exquisite communicator."

Dr. Heidi Heron

60. Easily Create Rapport—With Anyone!

Rapport is the unconscious connection we have with other people. When we have rapport, it is easier to communicate (even to disagree), understand, and to help influence or create a stable relationship.

Neurologically, we connect to others through what we see, hear, and feel. Neuro transmitters known as **mirror-neurons** start to identify when someone is similar to us; therefore, in NLP we use this to our advantage.

By **matching and mirroring** another person (or many people), you can purposefully trigger the mirror-neurons of someone else as you *become like them* for just a few moments. In simple terms, the unconscious mind of the person you are communicating with sees or hears the similar behaviours or traits and fires off a neurological signal telling the body/mind, "Ah, this person is like me. I like people who are like me!"

A few things you can match and mirror are body movements such as the crossing of legs and arms; tilting of the head; leaning in or back; where the body weight is centred; volume, pitch, and speed of the voice; key words; experiences; and concepts. Now, there are tips and tricks to building subtle rapport—if you overdo it, you'll get caught, and if you underdo it, it won't be effective.

61. Understand How Others Communicate

The basis of NLP is understanding how the mind works and communicates between the unconscious mind and the conscious mind. When we can understand how this works for us personally, we can also apply this information to others.

By simple observation, you can identify the program another person uses to communicate—and when you know this, you can feed it back to them. Essentially you can communicate directly through their filters of understanding. In NLP, we look at our five senses as more than just sensory input mechanisms. It's been found that we have a preferred mode within those five senses that we use the most.

So, not only do the skills of NLP allow you to identify a person's **Primary Representational System** (their preferred method of sensory based communication), but you can also start to understand the unconscious filters a person communicates with; in NLP, these filters are known as **Meta Programs**. By understanding how a person filters information, we can tailor our own communication to match their filters.

A few of these filters include considering the big picture vs. details, matching what they notice or mismatching what they notice, looking for what is good or looking for what is bad. Because each of us has our own **Model of the World**, NLP helps us to understand another person's model and communicate to them based on it.

62. Understand Others

In every single situation, we filter what is going on around us and inside of us based on our personal history, our memories, our beliefs, our values, and many other various unconscious filters. In NLP, we call these filters **Meta Programs**. They are the lenses we use to make sense of our world. For example, some people look for problems and some look for solutions, some people move toward what they want and others move away from what they don't want. Once we filter an event, we automatically distort, delete, and generalise it to make sense of it for ourselves. This is what is known as our **Model of the World**.

This filtering process explains why you and your best friend can have very different understandings of the exact same thing—because you have filtered it differently.

Everything we do, every behaviour we have, every decision we make and everything we say is based on this filtering process. It is understood that the majority of our filters were built or created during our **imprint stage**. According to developmental psychologist Dr. Morris Massey, the Imprint Stage begins at birth and continues to age 7; in this stage, we have very few filters in place and we start to create our beliefs, values, and various other programs, based on the people and environment around us. It is during this timeframe that the majority of our filters are created.

If I have a friend who is very clingy and wants to check in with me on a more-than-regular-basis, a few questions and some observations may be able to tell me that this friend has a fear of being abandoned. Now, I may not know why, and in my friendship, the why isn't necessarily important (even if I want to know!). What is important is that I can understand that this is a real fear of my friend's and I can be an even better friend by respecting her need to be with me.

NLP will provide you with many tools to understand each aspect of another person's **Model of the World**. You'll obtain listening, observing, and questioning techniques that will allow you to identify a person's beliefs, values, habits, and unconscious patterns of thought, emotions, and behaviours. With enough experience, you'll be able to understand more about a person in 30 seconds of observation that you may be able to do now with a 1-hour interview.

When you can understand someone in a deeper way, not only can you communicate more effectively with that person, but your underlying relationship also becomes deeper and stronger. This understanding of others will help you to truly respect their **Model of the World.**

63. Handle Difficult People

What makes people difficult? Mostly, we find that people are labelled as 'difficult' when they are different to us.

Everyone has a different **Model of the World**—and sometimes difficult people have a vastly different model than we do. In general life, we see people either avoiding or trying to challenge the difficult person. NLP looks at it a bit differently.

If someone is different to us and there is resistance in our communication, NLP sees this simply as a **lack of rapport**. So, to deal with that difficult person you can spend a few minutes building rapport and starting to understand where they are coming from.

Additionally, NLP has a few extra tools that will help you to be able to associate with that other person to gain an even better understanding of where they are coming from. called **Perceptual Positions** is an NLP tool that will help you to look from your perspective, their perspective, and a true objective perspective to gain a better understanding from various points of views. We also look at what the **Positive Intention** is behind any behaviour and understand this to be a part of a person's filtering process.

With the use of rapport, understanding a person's beliefs, values, positive intention and even by stepping into their shoes, handing those difficult people becomes a very easy task. In no time at all, NLP will help you become the person who gets along with everyone—easily!

64. Understand Yourself and Your Triggers

All communication—*interpersonal* (with others) and *intrapersonal* (with you)—starts with you. With NLP you can understand others in order to adapt to them, respect their model of the world, and better influence a positive outcome; however, the most important person to understand is yourself.

With NLP, you are able to better understand yourself and what your triggers are. Triggers might be **anchors** that activate a positive or negative response.

We filter information through our five senses and our various programs, including our history, beliefs, values, memories, and other unconscious filters. Everything we do and every emotion we have has some sort of neurological reason for it – we see, hear or feel something and it automatically releases a chemical or hormone, and we react depending on that.

Most of us go through life thinking, "well, this is just how I am," whether that be optimistic, anxious, positive, depressed, outgoing, slow, or anything else. But it's not 'just how you are' – it's how you've been programmed. Your **Model of the World** is based on the foundations of your programming. NLP will help you to understand what programs are running. And, of those programs, what programs are working, not working, outdated, redundant, or broken.

When we are communicating with others, we often react unconsciously due to what has been said or done or even how someone looks at us. These unconscious reactions are anchors and our behaviour is a direct reaction. When you can better understand yourself and the triggers in your life, you can communicate better.

For example, if I know that conflict causes me to retreat into myself, knowing this allows me to do better. I will know that I may need more time to explain myself, I may need to explain to someone what has just happened, or even to learn to handle conflict in a new and beneficial manner.

Additionally, if I know that I am prone to being very detailed, this gives me information to work with if I'm talking to someone who is more big-picture oriented. It gives me a choice of altering my style of communication or not. Yet another example is communicating with someone who has very different ideas or beliefs than I do. By first understanding my values and beliefs about myself, I can be more congruent when communicating with others. We have found that when people don't understand themselves it is easy to be swayed, influenced or manipulated in a way that is not useful or beneficial.

A presupposition of NLP is, "**When you know better, you can do better**." By identifying your own patterns, triggers, and anchors, you will be able to communicate more effectively with yourself and with others.

65. Develop Sensory Acuity Skills

Sensory acuity is the ability to have a keen awareness, specifically with what you see and hear. According to various studies, only 7% of communication comes from the verbal words you say; the remaining 93% is based on the voice and body.

You cannot *not* communicate: everything you do, every way you move, every intonation has some meaning. Over the years, psychology has taught us to pay attention to micro movements and to be aware of others. NLP takes this one step further to help you develop **sensory acuity** with others and yourself.

When you are sensory acute, you are observing and aware of subtle changes or effects of a person's movements and voice. This may be a twitching of the leg, rubbing of hands, squinting of the eyes, breathing, muscle tension, sighing, sweating, stammering, changing volume, pitch, or tempo, eye movements, or a range of other things.

While NLP teaches you to be aware of these things—unlike may non-verbal communication books or articles—NLP does not assign meaning to them. The meaning to everything is very personal and individual; sometimes the meaning changes in the moment. Along with sensory acuity, NLP teaches you how to **calibrate** for meaning. That is, NLP helps you to understand what these changes mean. And, instead of guessing or "mind-reading," NLP will assist you in either observing behaviour over time to ascertain meaning, or asking a question to gain more information/to better understand someone's behaviour at the moment.

Most people are unaware that a change has just occurred, so when you ask someone, "I just noticed you crossed your arms when talking about your boss, what do you think that means?" you are, in essence, asking them about an unconscious reaction and bringing it to their conscious awareness.

By being more sensory acute, not only will you start to pay more attention to the subtleties in a conversation, but you will also be more aware of and be able to respect someone's model of the world. In turn, this simple tool can mould you into an exquisite communicator.

66. Take Things Less Personally

We make decisions in a nano-second. These decisions are based on our history, our memories, our beliefs, and other filters. Some people are programmed to take everything personally – to make some sort of meaning about what someone did or said and make it about them.

Now, there isn't anything wrong with this unless it creates a conflict and interferes with confidence, self-belief, or your identity. Our patterns of emotions, behaviours, and thoughts were programmed in long ago, and NLP offers tools to help us change patterns that don't work for us.

While it's all well and good to say to someone, "Don't take it so personally," it is a completely different thing to not take it personally. We have beliefs that uphold our behaviours, so in order to change or alter a behaviour, we need to change a belief or concept about ourselves.

Sometimes these beliefs don't make any logical sense – which is because beliefs are not always logical. They connect somewhere in the past, but may or may not be relevant in today's world. For example, a person who got praise for doing well when they were little, or another person who was criticized and punished for any discrepancy, may both form a pattern of taking things personally.

One size does not fit all when it comes to patterns, beliefs or programs. However, if you do take things personally and that creates an interference, that pattern comes from somewhere. NLP will give you the insight into where it came from and how to change it.

There is a wonderful Polish proverb that we tend to relate back to NLP and our personal control: "Not my circus, not my monkeys." This is relevant in NLP because we do our best to respect someone else's model of the world without taking everything on board for ourselves.

So, the next time you start to take something personally – step back and think "not my circus, not my monkeys"

67. Get Out of Your Head and Come Back to Your Senses

Until you are about 4-5 years old you have very few filters; in fact, the **Imprint Stage** spans from birth to age 7 and this is where we absorb information (what do we then do with that information?). However, those years between birth to 4-5 years are spent mostly engrossed in our senses. We get to play, imagine, make up songs, pretend for hours and generally get swept up in the moment without much thought.

Can you remember that? Getting swept up in the moment without much thought? What a wonderful place that would be!

Somewhere around 4 or 5, when a child starts school, we move from being in our senses to being in our head. We are then taught to *think* and *pay attention* and *be aware*. Slowly, our sensory play ends. Thinking or being focused internally is a learned behaviour. And it is a behaviour that we needed to learn to efficiently navigate a world full of different offerings and choices. After all, thinking and analysing helps us to move forward in life, get things done, choose our path appropriately and be an adult. However, over-thinking, over-analysing, over-processing can create interferences and issues.

Being in your head too much can create patterns of perfection, a need for certainty, a sense of mindless superiority, procrastination, fear of failure – and the dreaded paralysis-by-analysis.

Again, thinking is important – but *not* thinking is more important.

The **conscious mind**—that is the part of your mind with which you think, analyse and reason with—makes up approximately 10% of your mind. The remainder is your **unconscious mind**. Your unconscious mind is responsible for your perceptions, emotions, storage of memories, creation of chemicals and hormones, and it runs your body.

Your unconscious mind is currently processing what you are reading, making sense of it, relating this to what you've learned in the past, and considering how it might be useful in the future; it's also digesting the last meal you had, producing saliva, beating your heart, compressing and expanding your lungs, producing and distributing chemicals, blinking your eyes, swallowing pre-mentioned saliva, and producing antibodies to keep you well. All of this happens in the span of a blink.

Can you recall a time when you wanted to remember a quote you read from a book – you know what it was about, but can't remember the exact words? But, you know what book it was, and that it was toward the back of the book, on the top of a left hand page? It's your unconscious mind that knows all of that. Your conscious mind only knows, "I want to remember this quote."

Even if you were to recall that quote immediately, it is still the unconscious mind that stores the quote and it is the unconscious mind that delivers it to the conscious mind.

Think of the conscious mind as the screen of a computer and the unconscious mind as the computer. It's the computer that stores and runs everything – the screen just shows you what is going on.

When we interview people who are successful at something, be it business, career, a hobby, relationships, life—anything really! most of them tell us that they don't spend much time dwelling or ruminating over anything. They think, process—tap into their body (head, heart, gut, brain)—and make a decision and move on.

We train a lot of entrepreneurs and business leaders and many of them start their NLP journey by being in their mind a lot. But, after making friends with their vast and friendly unconscious mind they find out that less is often times more: less thinking, less worrying, less need for control brings *more* confidence, *more* energy, *more* time, *more* freedom, and *more* peace of mind.

68. Manage Your Internal Dialogue

It has been said that we have between 50,000-70,000 thoughts per day. That equates to between 35-48 thoughts per minute! Your internal dialogue is a steady stream of consciousness that flickers between the past, present and future; concepts, ideas, pictures, sounds and feelings.

Our mind is on the go 24 hours a day. Even while we sleep our mind is on, just in a different way.

We get asked one question often 'how do you stop your mind' – and for the average person, the answer is simple: **you don't.** In fact, in daily life, you don't want to stop your internal dialogue, you want to **manage** it.

There are times that it is useful to stop your mind and the internal chatter, and that would be during a meditative state; even after much practice not many people get to a space of internal silence. In daily life, internal silence would not be a good thing. We need our inner chatter, our inner thoughts, our internal dialogue and conscious mind to be on and working for us.

What we don't want however, is for us to be working for our unconscious mind. This happens if our mind is filled with so much chatter that distracts us from the task at hand, or if it is primarily negative in nature, fearful or if there are self-sabotaging patterns that take over productive strategies. We find this happening when people are stressed or worried about something, the mind chatter can be so loud, it is hard to hear yourself think!

In Buddhism, they call the unsettled, restless, uncontrollable mind the **monkey mind**. Buddha described the human mind as being filled with drunken monkeys jumping around, screeching, chattering and carrying on endlessly. Think about a recent time when you were possibly overwhelmed or were worrying about something. Were you able to stay on track with one thought or activity? Probably not – your monkey mind was probably in full swing.

We all have a monkey mind; some are louder or drunker than others, calling for our attention, especially if there is fear involved. In a fear-based mind, the monkey mind points out all the imminent dangers, pitfalls, and what could potentially go wrong.

Our drunken monkeys can be hiding in plain sight. The fear of failure, fear of success, need for control, perfectionism, pessimism, naysayer mind – these are all drunken monkeys trying to control us.

In NLP, we have the following presupposition: **"You are in charge of your mind, and therefore your results."** We recognise thoughts as just thoughts – not the truth, but a bias. When we can view a thought as merely a thought, it takes the power out of it.

Let's look at it this way: every thought you have automatically creates an immediate chemical reaction which produces a feeling, and this feeling directly leads to an action (even inaction is an action), which in turn leads to the next thought.

Thought – Feeling – Action – Thought – Feeling – Action – Thought -Feeling – Action, ad nauseam.

Therefore, to truly manage your internal dialogue, you need to manage the feeling that is created from the thought, and to do this, you first need to be aware of the triggers you have in life that create the feelings.

NLP contains many tools to help you do just that. You will learn how to recode your thoughts using **submodalities**, change a reaction to a stimulus by **collapsing anchors**, amend unresourceful beliefs with **timeline techniques**.

Let's take an example of a person who has a fear of failure, which in turn has created a need for perfection and a need to be in control. This in turn may create procrastination – because if something is not perfect and if they aren't in control, then they may fail – so it's better to not start something than fail. That's the thinking at least.

Unconsciously, there is a thought to do X, which leads to a feeling of, 'I might not get this right,' which leads to procrastination or inaction.

Using NLP, we can use a tool like **Unconscious Pattern Change** which utilises a person's timeline to identify where a pattern of emotion, behaviour or thought comes from. We can then change the neurological and biochemical trigger that has been created. In this example, the fear of failure may have come from when the person was 3-years-old and they spilled a glass of milk and got in trouble for it. Something as benign and innocent as a small child being scolded for a behaviour they may or may not have been in control of is enough to create a lifetime pattern that gets in our way.

Before you can even start to change these emotional triggers from your thoughts, it is important to begin to simply be aware of the thoughts you are having. This awareness creates a **pattern interrupt** which can lead to a different outcome. Instead of: thought – fear – inaction, it can become Thought – fear – awareness – new thought – new feeling

Start with being aware of your thoughts and then move to the understanding that they are just thoughts and nothing more than that. With this simple insight, the thoughts become just a rumour and we can start to short circuit the old neurological patterns and create new ones.

69. Change Your Beliefs

What do you believe to be true in your world? True about yourself, your life, the world around you, other people, communication, money, time, aging, relationships? You may not realize it, but you have beliefs about everything. Everything!

A belief is a truth you hold with emotions behind it.

The majority of our beliefs were developed during the imprint stage in life between birth and the age of 7, and some were learned later in life; you may have even created a new belief today!

We learn our beliefs through the world around us, and our beliefs make up a very large part of our model of the world. Most of the beliefs you have support you in your life, and some hold you back.

If you've ever asked the question, "why do I do x?" the simple answer is: **because you have a belief that supports that behaviour**. And, to truly change that behaviour, you need to address the belief behind it. Not all of our beliefs make logical sense, and most of the time we may not be consciously aware of what we believe.

Whilst our beliefs are largely unconscious, NLP provides a variety of tools to help you to identify your beliefs, and even more to change them. Namely, you will learn NLP techniques including **unconscious pattern change** to change a belief at the root cause, **submodalities** to alter the unconscious coding of a belief, **mapping across meta programs** to model the belief patterns from another area of your life and **reimprinting** to add resources to your younger self and empower the opportunity for new beliefs.

For example, we worked with a gentleman who was having issues with money. Whatever he did, whatever he earned, whatever he spent was always gone before the month was up. When we dove into the unconscious patterns that were connected to this, he identified a belief that, "I can't be more well off than my family or friends – if they go without, I have to, too."

This wasn't something that he had ever consciously thought of, but the pattern in his life was very strong and pervasive.

In NLP, identifying the belief isn't enough. We want to actually change beliefs that are interferences to our desired states. Some of the NLP processes that you'll learn include unconscious pattern change, reimprinting, change personal history, parts integration, neurological levels alignment, submodality belief change, colliding and colluding beliefs, belief change cycle, and many more!

70. Manage Your State

A state is a mood or an emotion, and you are in charge of your mood, even if it doesn't feel like that at times! NLP will help you to be able to better manage your states and be more in control of your moods because you will learn skills to be more aware of your current state and techniques to change your mood to a more resourceful one

Everything happens twice in life; first in our imagination and then in reality. Therefore, your state actually starts well before reality happens. If you think about a meeting you are going to have tomorrow and get excited about it, that is the beginning of your state, your mood and your psychology. If, however, you get frustrated thinking about the meeting, then that is the beginning of how you enter the meeting.

There are two main components of a state: 1) what is happening inside of your body and 2) what is happening outside your mind.

Inside your body starts with your mind and the cascade of chemicals produced by your brain. These chemicals are receptors or transmitters of emotions which tap into the programs of your present and past experiences. The direct output of these chemicals is your physiology (your body posture, facial expression, muscle tension, eye movement, perspiration, voice tempo, tone, volume, etc.), and the direct output of your physiology is your mood or state.

When you change even one aspect of your physiology, your state must start to change, even if just a little. This is why when someone is sad or near tears they often look *up*. Or to get motivated or energised about something, someone may stand up or sit up. And to relax, we often lean back, lay down or otherwise fold in on ourselves.

The mind and body are connected, and help you to manage your state. To truly be in charge of your state however, you'll need to develop personal self-sensory acuity skills to become aware of your current mood or state.

71. Influence the State of Others

Have you ever heard the saying, "Enthusiasm is contagious"? Or, have you ever walked into a room where there is a disagreement going on? Or perhaps you have been in a kind of down mood and gone into a space with others and your mood has been lifted?

We have a natural way of influencing each other. It is nearly impossible to contain our state, mood or emotions to only ourselves. If you are happy chances are others around you will be too. If you are depressed, anxious, sad, annoyed, frustrated, hurt or angry, there is a good chance that your mood will rub off onto others, too.

NLP knows this and uses it to our advantage.

Armed with the concept of rapport, mirror neurons and synergy, you will be better equipped to influence the state of others by using NLP. Therefore, if you are a sales person and you want your potential client to be receptive to what you are selling, you can influence this state. If you are a parent and you want to help induce a sleepy state in your children at bedtime, you can influence that, too. If you are wanting to have a serious conversation with a silly friend; or a silly conversation with a serious friend, you can influence these states too.

That being said, the key word here is *influence.* When it comes to others, they are in charge of themselves just as you are in charge of you. With NLP, you cannot make someone do something; you can only be an influence. As the other saying goes, you can lead a horse to water, but you can't make him drink. With NLP, the leading part becomes an elegant dance!

72. Improve your Influence Skills

We each have our own way of seeing the world, and we like to be right. When you want to influence another person, you must understand how they see the world and get in that view with them, in order to help them see your perspective through their view of the world.

As we have said, a key word with a lot of NLP is *influence.* When you are influential you have the capacity to have an effect on the character, state, choice or behaviour of someone else. Trainers, managers, parents, sales professionals, customer services representatives, friends – we all want to have good influence skills at times.

Each of us is unconsciously governed by a variety of filters, through which we make sense of the world. When you can identify, understand and use the filters of another, that will in a sense mean you are unconsciously *speaking their language.* If you are speaking with someone who filters through images, you can use more visually-based language with them. If someone else needs details to make sense of a concept, you can provide them with the details they need. If another person requires a consequence for not following through on a task, you can help to provide that consequence.

Additionally, with NLP skills you will be able to identify *how* a person is thinking or processing information and you can use this to influence their thoughts.

When you can communicate and behave toward and with people in a way they unconsciously connect with, you will create a much better chance for them to not only see your point of view, but also be within the frame of their model of the world. You will learn that the more flexible you can be in your behaviours with other people, the more influential you will be.

73. Separate Behaviour From Intention

When you judge another person (and let's face it, we all judge other people), do you judge them based on the behaviours you have observed or the intention of those behaviours?

Interesting question, isn't it?

Most likely, you are basing your decision, judgement or assessment of someone on the behaviour you have witnessed. But, what if you were to understand that **people are not their behaviours?**

Think about a *bad* behaviour you recently had. Maybe you exhibited anger, or didn't go to the gym, or told a white lie.

Do those behaviours *make* you that person? Are you an angry person? A lazy person, a liar?

No. Those are your behaviours, *not* your identity.

But most of the time the only thing we, as outsiders, have to go on, is what we can observe – and that is most often someone's behaviours.

Did you know however, that every behaviour has a positive intention? That's right! With NLP, you will learn how to identify the positive intention behind any behaviour. This information will give you the understanding and insight into a person's beliefs, choices, filters, decisions and capabilities. Once you have a better understanding of what is happening unconsciously to create the behaviour you've witnessed, it makes it a lot easier to empathise, not judge, communicate and generally understand another person.

74. Identify How Others Process Information

To make sense of the world, our first filtering system is based on our five senses – what you see, hear, taste, touch and smell. Automatically, when something comes into your conscious or unconscious awareness, it triggers an internal response which ultimately leads to an outcome or behaviour, and eventually the mind stores the event as a memory.

Our memories then act as filters for future reference and for filtering the world around us.

Interestingly, the mind not only stores the whole memory, but also stores components of the memory in different ways. NLP has tapped into an idea and concept that was originated by American psychologist William James in the late 1800's. He hypothesised, and later identified that when our eyes move in different directions, we are actually accessing different types of information.

It seems that our brain dissects a memory and stores the visual, auditory, kinaesthetic (feeling) and internal dialogue (your own self talk) as separate components which add to our filtering process.

So, by watching someone's **Eye Accessing Cues,** you can identify how a person is processing information; for example, if they are making a decision, based on what they see, what they hear, what they feel or the logic they are telling themselves.

This non-verbal information helps in communication in a few ways.

First, it allows you to ask better questions; if you observe someone looking to their Auditory Recall space while saying, "I can't do that," then you can ask, "Who told you that?"

Second, it will help you to help others move out of stuck states; if someone is having a hard time creating goals and imagining the future and you see their eyes in the kinaesthetic space, you can ask them to look into the visual area and begin to dream and imagine.

Third, it will help you to identify key strategies for decision-making and more. If I want to influence someone in a positive way and, while they are deciding, I see their eyes move to their internal dialogue area, I want to appeal more to their logic. On the other hand, if their eyes move first to the kinaesthetic area, I may want to appeal more to their emotions.

Not only is watching a person's eye movements a great tool for improving communication by understanding *how* someone is processing information but it's also a great party trick that everyone should have!

75. Identify and Use Others' Strategies

When you have the ability to watch a person's eyes move, identify the eye pattern and follow a conversation at the same time, you will then be able to elegantly identify the unconscious *strategy* for how they do something.

In NLP, a *strategy* is a recipe or formula for how we process information for a response. We have strategies for absolutely everything in life: for how we learn, decide things, get motivated, communicate, make purchases, fall in love, everything! These strategies are also very unconscious to us; could you answer the question, "What process does your mind go through when you are learning something new?"

Probably not.

However, with NLP you can engage someone in a conversation about a time they learned something new and watch their eye patterns to see a sequence of accessing cues; you will start to elicit their strategy. The strategy will be 2-5 eye movements that start to loop.

When you know *how* a person unconsciously comes to their outcome, you can then play the strategy back to them in order to be more influential.

For example, if I want my child to easily start her homework, I can identify her motivation strategy for doing something she wants and then feeding that back to her. It may be that when she is motivated to play her eyes move first to Visual Construct, to Kinaesthetic to Visual Recall. Based on this, I could guess with pretty good accuracy (and if I'm wrong, that's OK, I just change my hypothesis), that she visually imagines what she's going to play, physically feels the fun of playing and then visually remembers a time like this before.

So, I can use my daughter's strategy to influence her; I could say something like, "Imagine what it will be like to be done with your homework for today, what will that feel like? Amazing I'm sure! Remember what that is like, to feel so good about being done for the day and having more time to do what you really want?"

Strategies in NLP are a very interesting topic. We take something that is so abstract and watch micro movements of the eyes to ascertain a sequence or recipe for how the mind makes order of something. This is a tool that you'll be able to use at home, at work, in sales, parenting, negotiations, with friends, and if you are really clever, with yourself!

76. Identify and Use the Communication Style of Others

Wouldn't it be wonderful to have a tool that would allow you to easily identify the preferred communication style of another, so that you can use their preferences when communicating with them?

We guarantee, it's a game-changer!

Each of us has our own distinct preference for how we absorb and make sense of the world around us, through the filters that make up our model of the world. Additionally, we have a way to disseminate information, too.

Often when we communicate with others, we use our own preferred communication style, in hopes that they will understand us fully and completely in the way we understand ourselves. That unfortunately doesn't always happen and the other person needs to translate what you've said into their own preferences. Often meaning gets lost in translation.

In NLP, we look at a variety of factors which make up a person's communication style. One of these factors includes the preferential *order* for processing information through the senses (visual, auditory, kinaesthetic, internal dialogue). While some schools of thought teach that you have a preferred communication sense, NLP argues you have *all* of them – in a preferred order!

Another factor is chunk size: does a person communicate in detail or with the big picture in mind? This is important information. Give a small-chunk-sized person) too big of a picture, and you'll lose them completely!

The way a person sorts for information is also important: are they communicating about the benefits or consequences? If you tell a consequences person about the benefits of something, it may not even compute! You see, the person who sorts for consequences will also be looking for consequences and information contrary to this may be deleted. When you know how a person filters information, you'll learn to use their style as a factor for communicating more effectively to them.

There are other factors, too, that NLP looks at, and when you are able to identify these aspects in terms of how a person communicates, you can match their style and preferences and communicate with them using their own filters—no unconscious translation required!

77. Find Out What Motivates Others

We humans are funny creatures. We tend to treat others how we want to be treated, which kind of makes sense – when it comes to morals, ethics and human needs. However, when it comes to what motivates us—what we believe or what we do—each of us is as different as our fingerprints.

With NLP, you will learn how to identify what motivates other people; from a communication standpoint, this is useful information. If you are a manager, parent, coach, teacher, personal trainer, doctor, or anyone who wants to motivate others, this skill will come in handy as you will have knowledge of how to use their unconscious programming to tap into their motivation

The motivations of people are largely dependent on their values and beliefs. Some example motivations might include time, money, gratitude, energy, touch, affection, love, responsibility, freedom, health, or a multitude of other possibilities.

With NLP, you will learn questioning and observing skills which will help you to identify the motivational drivers of others. Think about that for a moment. When you can identify how a person is motivated and you can use their filters to motivate them, who would you want to motivate and where would this be useful? Your children, staff, co-workers? How about in sales? Motivation comes in many forms, and you will have the ability to influence all aspects of motivation in others, and in yourself.

78. Identify What is Important to Others

As you were growing up and as you continued through life, certain aspects became important to you. In NLP, you will learn how the concept of importance relates to values.

We have values about everything: how you spend your time and money, relationships, communication, falling in love, the work you do, and so much more.

We learned many of our values at a very young age—somewhere within the Imprint Period and modelling, the stages of birth to 13 years old. They are a very unconscious aspect of ourselves and were learned by observing and modelling the people around us, our culture, religion, our teachers, our parents and ultimately, anyone deemed as important to us.

Our values are drivers for us—and when you can identify the values of others, you can communicate more effectively based on their values and in some instances, help them meet their values.

For example, if it is important for your spouse or partner to have independence, then you can communicate, behave and encourage them in a way that allows their value to be met.

79. Identify Someone Else's Beliefs

What do you believe to be true about climate change? How about owning a pet? Swimming in the ocean? Space travel? Your own personal growth and learning?

Just like so many other things in our world – we have beliefs about everything. Your beliefs are the truths you hold and the more emotionally charged they are, the more power and conviction they will have in your life.

For the most part, people tend to take beliefs for granted. We assume that because we're family or friends with others, because we work together, live together or share common experiences, we also share beliefs. This isn't always the case. In fact, oftentimes we have differing or even opposing beliefs to someone else, even if you are close to them.

By implementing observation and questioning skills, you will be able to identify the beliefs of others. When you are able to know the truths of other people, you can use this information to better respect their model of the world, motivate them and if necessary, invite change.

Unfortunately, beliefs are not always logical – but they are drivers to our behaviours; our beliefs are often the reason *why* we do what we do. Our guess is that easily 85-90% of the patterns of emotions, behaviours and beliefs that people have are derived from their beliefs. When you can ascertain another's beliefs, these unconscious gems open up a new awareness of the person's motives, directives and underlying intentions.

If you've ever asked someone (or yourself) the question *why*, next time ask, "What is your belief about that," and you'll tap into something wonderfully rich, interesting and possibly very powerful.

80. Respect Other People's Models of the World

If we could boil down the communication benefits of learning and using NLP, it would simply be to respect another person's model of the world.

You Must Learn NLP | 83

Each of us has our own model based on our memories, history, values, beliefs, senses and filters—and all of this gives us our different viewpoints, perspectives, responses and ideas. Wouldn't the world be a little boring if we all looked at it in the same way? Maybe that would be good sometimes, but when it comes to advancement, growth and longevity of our race, we need differences to flourish.

When you can respect someone else's model of the world, this means just that: you respect the view and by extension, the person as well. Respect the sameness and respect the difference. It doesn't mean you have to agree with it, live by it, or even understand it! Just respect it.

In real life, this means being more tolerant, patient, accepting and kind when someone thinks, acts, believes or behaves in a way we personally wouldn't. We have seen relationships flourish, careers evolve, sales increase, fights stop and love begin after someone learns NLP and really begins to embrace the aspect of respecting someone else's model of the world.

81. Find Out That There are Many Ways to do the Same Thing

In the late 1800's, a gentleman named Charles Duell was the head of the U.S. Patents department and it is understood that he tried to encourage the government to *shut it down* because, "Everything that can be invented has been invented." It's a good thing Mr. Duell didn't have NLP skills to help him be more influential!

Can you imagine that? At the turn of the century, if everything that could have been invented, had already been invented. This, is an example of a **fixed mindset:** there is only one way to do something.

When you learn NLP, you will be empowered to think outside of the square, to look for options, alternatives, and possibilities; this is otherwise known as the **growth mindset.**

An NLP presupposition states *the person with the most flexibility can control the situation*, and when we are talking about control here, we're talking about the ability to influence, persuade, entice, and promote choice. After all, **choice is always better than no choice.**

82. Understand the Psychology of Others

The foundation of NLP is rooted in psychology. When NLP was developed in the 1970's, it was based on modelling the excellence of a few psychologists at the time. Not only is psychology the study of behaviour and the mind, but we each also display our personal psychology. and aspects of our conscious and unconscious patterning.

With NLP, you will be able to better understand the psychology of others. As we've mentioned throughout this chapter, a person's mindset is made up of aspects such as beliefs, values, filters, memories, history, and more. All of this helps to shape and create our psychology.

From a psychological viewpoint, without needing to understand the complexities of diagnosis, you will instead be able to understand the underlying structure of anxiety, depression, fears, phobias, helplessness, stress, stuckness, and more. Additionally, you will better understand motivation, success, creativity, freedom, choice, and optimism with a clearer scope.

Not only will NLP help you to understand the psychology of others better, but you will also gain many tools to help you communicate more effectively, help someone change patterns of their psychology which might not be serving them and also build, enhance and tap into the positive psychology a person has.

Using NLP in Business

"A common theme in business is people. Sometimes business owners want us to help them with their business — we do this by helping them with their people."

Laureli Blyth

83. Create Business Goals and Plans For Success

Have you ever noticed that planning for business and personal goals tend to be two separate tasks? Even if the business is yours! This is because business is about more than just yourself, and sometimes people feel there is more at stake in a business. Sometimes there is.

With your NLP skills, you will be able to create an objective viewpoint of your business, your role in it, who else is or needs to be involved and how it affects others. Unlike many personal goals, your business goals almost always involve others.

NLP contains many tools to help you get out of your emotional/personal mindset and more critically create business goals that are realistic, achievable, and manageable. NLP provides steps along the way and added benefits of accessing and building resources – which might include other people!

The **Well-Formed Outcome** is the best of the NLP goal setting tools, and implementing the **Perceptual Positions Exercise** will let you look at your goals and business from different perspectives. **The Disney Planning Process** will help you to on board you own *personal dreamer, realist* and *critic* in your goal planning process. Using a **Goal in the Future** will help your unconscious mind connect with your goals in a deeper and more meaningful way. All the goal setting tools from your NLP toolbox will set you and your business goals and plans up for success!

84. Create Training Programs Based on Psychological Needs

Have you ever been to a time management course? This is just one example of most training programs out there that teach the skills of already-successful people to others who don't have the mindset for it in the first place.

Let's take the time management course as an example. I've yet to find a *standard* time management course that doesn't teach students to prioritise, plan out time, and organise your day. And yes, this is what good time managers do, so it would be a reasonable option to learn such concepts. But, if the people sitting in the training had the mindset to do those tasks, they wouldn't be sitting in a classroom learning *all over again* the steps to a successful day.

This is where the aspects of NLP come in extremely useful in training. Sure, people need to be trained or taught the 'how,' but what is most often missing in soft-skill type training (anything to do with people) is the mindset.

When was the last time you saw a time management workshop and they talked about your beliefs and mindset? Have you ever heard a trainer sharing Time Management skills say that it is absolutely okay to procrastinate, be deadline-driven and do your best work at the last minute?

Probably not.

However, if you come to one of our Time Management workshops t we run for our corporate clients, you will learn just that.

You will learn a **modelling** technique that allows you to unpack another person's unconscious patterns and transform that knowledge into an actionable training program. We do it regularly.

For example, we might be asked to create a training program for an engineering company's sales team. Our first step would be to interview and model some of their top sales professionals, and even someone from another company if we can, to identify the psychology they use to become the top sales people. After this, we look for the common denominators between them—similar beliefs, values, mindset, unconscious filters, internal dialogue—and we find our map of success.

This information turns into a dynamic training program based on the psychological needs of the participants. Couple this with what is already being trained from a functional standpoint, and you have a winning combination!

85. Improve Recruitment Strategies

Employee retention can be greatly improved by hiring the right people in the first place. Unfortunately, too many old-school recruitment techniques are still being used. I cringe whenever I hear the question, "What do you think your strengths and weakness are," or, "Give me an example in a previous job when you X happen." Capability and behaviour-based interviews don't always result in the best candidates.

Recruitment is generally characterised by soliciting resumes, looking through those resumes for someone who has the skillset or background that you are looking for, and interviewing your potential candidates for the right fit.

What does that mean? The right fit? Is that "right" in terms of skills or person? Skills can be taught; mindset is a harder thing to train. Have you ever seen the most competent and skilled person hired for the job, but they still didn't fit somehow? That's mindset.

With NLP, we look at a variety of unconscious filters that you can easily identify while talking to another person—and we match those to the filters that might be required for the job, the workplace, the team and the management.

Instead of asking about a behavioural aspect, ask, "Tell me about an aspect of your current/past job that you truly enjoyed" instead; this will give you insight into the person's mindset and help you choose a better candidate. NLP will provide you with skills and knowledge about how to create a recruitment plan for your business to ensure the right-minded person with the right skills is being hired.

86. Separate Self From Business

In our coaching practices, we work with and train many business professionals and entrepreneurs. When we meet someone who is struggling with boundaries, balance and flow in their life, we have found a common theme—sometimes people associate themselves too personally with their business. 'They' are the business, rather than being themselves.

But, that's not necessarily true. Your job, your business, your hobbies—they are just that: a job, a business, a hobby.

NLP will help you to dissociate personally from your business and step into a more objective role where you can find breathing space, make better choices and take it all less personally.

87. Manage Others More Effectively

Managing and leading others is sometimes a challenging task, especially if you have a team of people who are quite different from one another. Effective management skills start with a better understanding of the people on your team, and by that, we mean understanding their beliefs, values, motivation, what pushes their buttons and slows them down, and how to manage that person in the way they need to be directed.

Management is an individual game; each person generally needs to be lead in a slightly different way because of his or her model of the world. The ultimate respect you can give to someone is when you realise you need to get the same outcome for the whole team, but lead people differently to arrive at the same destination.

Unfortunately, the business world doesn't do a good job of training people to be managers. People get promoted because they were good at their previous job, or they start their own company, or create their own team— and boom! They are a manager. The skills of NLP will help you to fast-track your interpersonal communication skills, coaching abilities and leadership qualities!

88. Manage Your State/Mood

Unless you work alone in a silo, it is useful to have your emotions and mood in check. From an NLP perspective, your mood and emotions at any point in time is known as your **state**, and it changes regularly.

If you are managing or leading people, selling, influencing, helping or otherwise working with people, your state is important. Studies have shown that the moods of others can easily be passed from person to person—and negative emotions win out over positives ones nearly every time!

If you want others around you to be upbeat, positive, creative or productive, then it would make sense that you would want to be the model of that yourself. Now, let's face it, it's not always possible to be in a good mood. In fact, bad moods can actually be useful.

Anger, frustration, challenged, sad, worried—they are all useful in some context. In the right conditions, anger demonstrates that you are setting boundaries, that your values have been dismissed or a line of some sort has been crossed. But to hold onto anger for hours, or days is unuseful.

You are in charge of your mind, and therefore your results. NLP will help you to be more aware of the states you are having – and when such states are unproductive for you or for the people around you. And, more importantly, NLP will teach you how to change the state you are experiencing to transform it into something that is more useful and resourceful.

89. Improve your Leadership Skills

Business could easily be boiled down to one critical skill: leadership. This includes leadership of your team, your clients, your community and most importantly, leadership of yourself.

There is a debate in the world: "Is leadership a trait that can be learned?" Our answer based on NLP is **absolutely, yes!** The mere notion that leadership is a trait to begin with is what brings this concept into question. However, what if leadership were a skill versus a trait? Anyone can learn a skill! But in fact, using NLP, anyone can also create a trait!

By understanding how others communicate, process information, make decisions, get motivated, need information delivered and how they act based on their programs creates a dynamic landscape for leadership skills to be developed.

Now, there isn't one single way to lead; people need to be lead in different ways. NLP will help you to gain the skills to understand the needs of yourself others and so you can adapt your leadership style to fit anyone you lead.

90. Improve Customer Service Skills

We're sure you've heard the phrase, "the customer is always right," but is that really true? Of course not! But, from an NLP angle, the *way* the customer sees something is right, *for them.*

When an event happens, we filter this information through a set of criteria which include your beliefs, values, history, expectations, memories, etc. After that, your mind automatically fits what has just happened into your own model of the world by distorting, deleting and generalising information; this is how each of us has our own opinions, thoughts and ideas about the same thing.

NLP will help you to improve your customer service skills, not by making the customers right all the time, but by making how they see something right. If a customer, for example, is unhappy with something, you will be able to get more specifics about what it is, how they have come to that conclusion and what needs to happen to fix the situation—therefore, you have more skills at your disposal to create a happier customer.

Customer service isn't only something that happens when a customer is upset—it is simply a way of treating our clients. Each client has their own needs, values, expectations and desires; through sensory acuity and observation skills, questioning techniques and filtering tools, you will be able to better understand what your client needs, how they need it and how you can best serve your customer for long-term rewards, retention and referrals.

91. Use NLP in Marketing

Do you like being sold to?

Nope, us neither. Nor do most people. But so many marketing and sales campaigns tend to do too much direct selling, and not enough influencing. Marketing, after all, should create a strong call to action where the sales process can begin.

Using NLP as a tool to market your services and products, you'll be delving into the psychology of a person's mind to influence their decisions. Now, that being said, NLP can't make someone purchase something they don't actually desire, but if someone is looking for what you are selling, using NLP will help you be more effective at marketing your wares.

Marketing using NLP includes tapping into the unconscious **meta programs** that run behind the scenes of the mind. You will be appealing to their preferred representational system, speaking in different chunk sizes, identifying their buying strategy, finding if they are motivated toward benefits or consequences, seeing if they need internal or external validation, determining if they want something similar or different to what they've had in the past and many other unconscious filters.

With NLP, you'll have an easy way to identify the psychological needs of your prospective customers to be more successful at marketing your services and products to them. And also, to be more successful and better at customer service.

92. Improve Your Training and Presentation Skills

A very dynamic way to use your NLP skills is to improve your training and presentation skills. In fact, we offer a 14-day course (Level 3), that teaches you how to use NLP as a tool for training and presentations.

Training and presenting is different than teaching, consulting or coaching. Yet, we find that so many people attempt to train others in the same way as they would teach, consult or coach. It generally doesn't work very well for long-term results.

Teaching is sometimes too one-way from the front of the classroom back, for example. Consulting is often too directive, not allowing the learner to actually engage and learn. Coaching is often either too instruction-based (like sports coaching), or too collaborative (like personal coaching) for learning to transpire.

Training however, from an NLP perspective, is a two-way approach to disseminating information that can be understood by the mind and processed by the body, making it a robust, creative and engaging process.

With NLP as a tool for training and presenting, you will not only be using a person (or a group's) learning style, you will also be delivering in a way, order and fashion that will engage everyone. You will also utilise metaphors as a teaching aid (which are SO much more effective than Power Point!), spatial anchors to solidify concepts and create states, rapport to create connection and group cohesion, non-verbal communication skills to train the unconscious mind, nested loops to bring home a point—all while delivering information at different neuro-logical levels and different meta program dichotomies to reach every person in your audience.

At the end of the day, people learn the same information in different ways, at different speeds with different desires. NLP will help you to meet the needs of each of your students so you can help them to learn and embody their learning.

93. Set Yourself Up for More Success

Regardless of what kind of business you are in, NLP helps you set yourself up for more success. It doesn't matter if you own a business, are a receptionist, sales person, parent, artist, coach, trainer, shelf-stocker—you are in charge of your mind. A couple of years ago, Sarah completed our NLP Level 1 trainings with zero intention to use it in her job because, "Well, I'm just an administrator"; her intention was simply to help herself communicate better, run her mind/body more effectively and improve her relationships.

Well, she did all of that—and more!

With NLP, you'll not only learn a superb goal-setting tool, you'll also be able to adjust your behaviours, thoughts and beliefs to match the outcome you want. Sarah learned that in her personal life, when she was focusing on what she wanted and when she addressed any blocks or limitations that were stopping her. So, she decided to try her hand at using NLP at work.

She set a Success Goal; her first goal was for others to give her verbal feedback about her improved performance. In reality, she didn't change her performance at all – she changed her attitude toward her performance! In turn, she began getting positive feedback. Her next goal was to get a promotion to a Senior Administration role; within a few months, she got that! Sarah continued to the Level 2 NLP training, learned about the Disney Planning Process and decided it was time to fast-track her work success, since she hadn't prioritised it earlier in her career. She's recently been promoted again, this time into the marketing department of her company – she is working directly for the Senior Manager, learning a lot and using her NLP skills every day in her work, and for herself.

Whatever you put your mind to, you can achieve—and with NLP you can make sure your success psychology is aligned with what you desire!

94. Improve Your Communication Skills

Do you think you are a good communicator? We are sure you are—most people are good communicators. Some people are horrific—they don't pay attention, they mind-read, they don't listen, they make assumptions, they aren't present mentally or emotionally in conversations; I think we've all communicated with someone like that.

Interestingly, it generally isn't the horrific communicators who are interested in NLP in the first place! After all, to improve your communication skills, you have to first know that they need to be improved and be open to learning.

Often, horrific communicators a) don't know they are horrific because well, they aren't paying attention and b) they aren't open to learning or changing their ways.

We find the people who enter our NLP Training room are much different. They are already good communicators, like you! And they desire to be *even better!* We're then looking at creating superb, excellent, exceptional, even triumphant communication skills!

We know that one of the main benefits of NLP as a communication skill is that it teaches you how to become more aware of others, and within that comes the skills of listening, questioning, investigating, supporting, connecting, empathy and really hearing and understanding others. In turn, this allows you to apply skills to verbally and non-verbally communicate in a way that is most appropriate to your audience. You can communicate to others *how* they will best process your message.

All of this together creates skills that will help you to be an exquisite communicator!!!

95. Identify and Align Company Values

If you are working in a position where you have a voice in the direction of the company, you can use your NLP skills to identify and align yourself with the company values. If you have your own company, this is very important too; a lot of entrepreneurs use their own personal values for their business, yet it is a very separate entity which warrants values of its own.

When we speak about values from an NLP perspective, we are talking about "what is important to you." So, when we are speaking about the Values of a company—the company becomes the entity of "you." This could also be "team" or "project" values—which might be slightly different than the company as a whole.

When you are aware of the values of your company, then you will be able to direct the company toward aligning the message of these values to your employees, customers, shareholders and community at large. The message you deliver through your marketing can be consistent, toward your objectives and can illustrate a clear message about who the company is and what it stands for.

Brand marketing, awareness and competency comes from strength in knowing about and being aligned to values. For example, Apple has some of the following values: (remember: what is important to Apple) simplicity, ownership and control of their technology, significant contribution, important and meaningful projects, collaboration to innovate, excellence and honesty.

Even if you aren't a fan of Apple, they exemplify these values everywhere you look because they are aligned to them. Being aligned means that the behaviours of the employees meet the values, the capability to deliver on these values is present, the beliefs of the company, teams, individuals, etc. are in sponsorship of these values and the identity is also demonstrating the values.

Your NLP skills will not only help you to identify the values of a company, but you will also be able to identify the incongruences and misalignments to create change at a cultural level within the organisation.

96. Develop Skills for Change Management

Change is one of the most inevitable aspects of life; we all know how to change—we may not always like it, but we can do it. To have the skills to facilitate the management of change is a whole new skillset for people.

With your skills of NLP, you will be able to manage the process of change for yourself and others within a business. Because everyone is programmed a little differently, we each respond to change in a different way. NLP manages this process by taking into consideration the similarities and differences between the message being communicated and *how* it is communicated to different people, teams, cultures, etc.

One of the presuppositions of NLP is to **respect another person's model of the world**. From a change management perspective, this means understanding that people are different from each other and one message doesn't suffice when speaking to a team or large group.

A fundamental tool used within change management is NLP's Meta Programs. Meta Programs are the unconscious filters we each have which help make sense of our world. You will learn how to identify the Meta Programs of others and how best to communicate toward those programs in order to facilitate change in a more cohesive manner.

For example, some people have an instant convincer strategy. That is, you tell them what is happening and why and they agree, comply with the changes instantly. Others have an over-time or a number-of-times convincer strategy. These people need a message delivered consistently either over time or a number of time before they will trust and change. Other people still have a never-convinced strategy and until they are appeased in different way will balk at change and may not adapt easily. Even with this last category, there are other Meta Programs which will influence change, create safety, and encourage the modification of attitude, behaviours, beliefs and sometimes identity.

97. Improve Your Conflict Resolution

Do you know anyone who loves conflict? We don't. We know people who handle conflict very well, and some people seem to live for the drama that conflict creates because it may somehow give them power; but we don't know anyone who really loves (or even likes) conflict. Sure, it is often a natural part of life, but that doesn't mean people like it.

Luckily, the skills of NLP will set you up for success in resolving conflicts. This is useful when you are in a conflict or even if you are mediating conflict between others.

Some of the tools from NLP that you will learn and use include: **perceptual positions**, to understand from another's point of view; **dissociation**, to step out of taking something personally; **separating behaviour from intention**, used to identify why the conflict exists on a higher level; **rapport**, to create a cohesive relationship even with a disagreement; **meta model**, which are questions to gain clarity; **meta questions**, to gain even more understanding of what is happening below the surface; **meta programs**, o identify the best way to communicate, influence, negotiate, manage, facilitate understanding in others; and **respecting another person's model of the world**, which might help you to learn something new and see a change that you need to create to resolve the conflict.

Although a person may not like conflict, the tools and skills of NLP will help you be adept at managing conflict resolution.

98. Effectively Manage Stress

Until around the 1960's, *stress* was a word that was primarily used for structural engineering. They would test the amount of stress a building, bridge or road could withstand before it became distressed. Now, *stress* is a term we use regularly and a physical condition most of us understand all too well.

Luckily, with the use of NLP you will be able to identify your triggers that create stress in your life and techniques to alleviate the stress if you desire. In the workplace, this is a great skill to have so that you can reduce your stress levels and have more energy and choice for what is important to you. Internal and external influences create stress type states, to which we generally react negatively.

High blood pressure, headaches, body aches, ulcers and more have been known to be caused by stress. From an NLP perspective, you will come to clearly understand two things: 1) every behaviour has a positive intention and 2) you are in charge of your mind and therefore your results.

You will learn how to identify what creates stress and what the mind/body connection is attempting to communicate to you through the stress mechanism. Using NLP tools to help yourself manage stress will help you to be more clear-minded, flexible, calm and in control.

99. Give More Effective Feedback

We often ask people, "Do you often know what someone else could do to improve their performance?" and the answer is yes. However, when we go on to ask, "Are you easily able to give people that feedback?" the answer changes.

So, whilst most people can observe others and know what they need to do to improve, sharing the information is a different story. We think this has to do with a discomfort with conflict. However, if you are in a management, leadership or training type of role, this might be an imperative part of your job. Imagine for a moment that no one ever gave you feedback. Would you have learned as much as you now know?

Feedback is a critical part of learning and growth. With NLP, you will learn how different people will respond to feedback so you can deliver feedback confidently in the manner they need to hear it—and will be most useful to them.

To do this, you'll be learning more about how to identify the unconscious filters of a person. For example, some people are more prone to filtering with emotions and others will filter with thought first. A person who filters through emotions may need a softer approach to feedback, while the person who filters through thought may just need direct feedback without the fluff.

Because everyone is different, sometimes giving feedback is challenging, but with NLP it never needs to be difficult.

100. Learn to Receive Feedback

The other side of being able to give feedback is being able to receive it. This lends itself to the debate between a **fixed** and **growth mindset**. A person with a fixed mindset will be less open and more reluctant to feedback, criticism and improvement. A growth mindset however, is more inviting to learning, challenges and being open to growth.

From our research, we've found that people don't like to receive feedback because they feel that it's somehow a judgement of them personally. What if, however, you employed the NLP presupposition that there is no failure, only feedback. What if feedback was an external mechanism to help you to continually improve? And what if that feedback helped you to be an even better version of yourself?

Not only will NLP help you to reframe, or look at feedback in a different way, but you will also be able to boost your levels of confidence and self-esteem to be able to be more open and willing to accept feedback.

101. Improve Your Time Management Skills

Have you ever been to a time management course? Generally, they teach skills and strategies to better manage your time. It might include goal-setting, prioritising, delegating, etc. However, have you ever met someone who implements these skills, yet still struggles with managing their time?

Of course you have!

Time management is much less about the strategies you put into place and more about the mindset you have about time.

If you have underlying beliefs such as, "I'm always late, I procrastinate, I have too much to do, I do my best work at the last minute," or anything similar, no matter what time management strategies you use, your unconscious patterns will override your attempts to manage your time.

Similarly, if you have behaviours such as not being able to say no, multi-tasking or perfectionism, the strategies you learn about managing time will generally not work.

This is where NLP comes in. With NLP, you'll be able to change beliefs that don't serve you, create new behaviours that are aligned with you want to do and understand how you best process information so you can work to your strengths.

What if you were to learn that procrastination and doing excellent work at the last minute could actually be strengths? If you are prone to those behaviours or beliefs, they actually might work in your favour once you embrace them instead of work against or around them.

We have seen so many people greatly benefit from managing their time through their own psychology vs. time management strategies. After all, when you give yourself permission to complete a task or project in a way that feels most natural to you, you are more likely to do your best. If you are following a strategy, that strategy may be time effective, but it may squander your creative energy and natural problem solving skills. We have always found productivity and success are best managed with your own natural style.

102. Better Understand Others

In business or in the workplace, there are so many different people that you communicate with. Anyone you see, email, call, Skype or otherwise encounter during the day is someone you have an influence over, regardless of your job, role or purpose.

Communication skills are what NLP is best known for, and you will be gaining so many tools that will help you to understand others. This will come from observing and actually listening to others. When you listen, you are listening more for *how* someone says something versus the story they are telling. Now, of course, listen to the story your client is telling you – but even more important is *how* they are telling you.

From the words, tonality, emphasis and other non-verbal cues, you will be able to identify another person's unconscious patterns of how they make sense of the world. This will give you more information to better communicate with them, or about them.

103. Influence Outcomes More Effectively

In your work, you may be responsible for achieving outcomes, either personally or as a team. Using your NLP tools, you will be able to influence outcomes more effectively.

When you can understand your teammates, customers, supplier, colleagues and others you work with, you can deliver a message to them in the manner they need it. Additionally, you will learn through NLP a variety of influential language patterns that have the ability to communicate more on an unconscious level.

These include skills such as metaphors, sleight of mouth, verb changes, identifying full belief statement, temporal phrases, tag questions, embedded questions, the Milton Model, negative commands and something strangely-named subordinate clauses of time. These tools were modelled from hypnotherapist Dr Milton Erickson. He was known for using therapeutic metaphors and ambiguity to create change within the unconscious mind. Milton Erickson believed that the unconscious mind would resist authoritarian suggestions, and instead he opted for *artful vagueness.*

The words we use begin to paint a picture for someone else. When you know what words to choose for specific people in specific contexts, you will become better at influencing outcomes.

104. Create Work/Life Integration

Do you have balance in your life? Work/life balance? Not many people do. We don't work and live in a balanced way. Generally, people work for 40-60 hours per week, have 50 or so hours to live, socialise, eat, study and play and we're asleep the rest of the time. That's not balance.

In the early 2000's, the concept of *Work/Life Balance* became all the buzz. But, as we've already looked at, balance was doomed from the start!

What if, instead of balance you sought work/life integration? More and more, people and companies (and countries!) are understanding that flexible work hours, telecommuting, and creating more workplace flexibility creates better employees and a better workplace.

In 2015, Denmark was rated the top country for work/life integration; they deem their success in many aspects of their citizens' balance to working short weeks and having family-friendly workplaces. Sweden has a 30-hour workweek or 6-hour workday to ensure employees have adequate time with their family, friends and themselves.

NLP can help you create a mindset of productivity and leisure. This means, when you are working you can be working efficiently and productively to do your job in a very time effective manner; when the workday is done, you can switch gears into more of a leisure mode—whatever that means for you.

The olden day rules of 40+ hours a week, being chained to a desk and golden handcuffs, do not need to exist anymore. In fact, more people than ever before are choosing to have a job versus a career. With NLP, you will be able to identify the values you have of a job, career, leisure time and personal time to make sure you get your values met.

What if a job was all you needed to create an income stream in order to get your life values met? For most people, this would mean they would spend more time doing what they enjoy and integrating their work and life into a harmony of sorts.

105. Transform Limiting Beliefs About Money

We have met people around the world who have conscious desires to create wealth, live with an abundance of money and know that although money doesn't buy them happiness, it can buy them nice stuff! However, so many people also have conflicting or colluding beliefs that do not align to their financial success.

Have you ever heard things like this: "Money is the root of all evil," "Good people live with little," ""Being rich is a sin," and/or, "I don't deserve to be financially free"?

Your beliefs are your truths in life and if you have a belief that is disempowering your desires, you will continue to be disempowered.

Many years ago, I worked with a client who truly desired financial independence; when we worked with his unconscious patterns and beliefs he remembered being just a young kid in church listening to the priest talking about the evils of money, and he quoted a piece of scripture that says, "It's harder for a rich man to get into heaven than for a camel to pass through the eye of a needle." As a child, we are open to most everything that comes into our awareness and will create beliefs if we hear or see something that comes from someone of importance or authority to us—without knowing if it is right or wrong.

Our patterns of emotions, behaviours and beliefs come from somewhere in our past. With NLP, you can transform these old beliefs to align them with your desires. You can change your thinking, mindset and beliefs from unresourceful to useful beliefs that will help you to create and keep more money, wealth and prosperity in your life, career, company or investments.

106. Remove Barriers to Success

We all want to be successful. I haven't met anyone yet that says, 'Nah, I'll just take averagely unsuccessful." Success feels good. It's desirable! At the end of the day, success is defined however *you* want it to be, for you. And, although we all want to be successful, why isn't everyone successful?

Largely, it comes down to the programming and mindset that a person has. If you have self-belief and confidence in yourself and your abilities, there is a good chance that you'll be *more* successful. If you have self-doubt and lack confidence, there is a good chance that you'll be *less* successful.

So, what is it really that stands between more and less success?

You.

Each of us has our own model of the world, which is made up of our history, memories, beliefs, values and a whole host of unconscious filters, known as **Meta Programs**. It is the combination of these aspects that creates our basis of personality, drive, motivation, self-concept, and, at the end of the day, our success.

With NLP, you will be able to identify any barriers or blocks to your success, and you will learn strategies to change these. For example, some people block their success in some aspects of life by comparing and judging themselves with others. Some other people have patterns of perfectionism or procrastination or all-or-nothing thinking that gets in the way of success. And some people have a fear of failure (or fear of success) that holds them back. There could be thousands of different patterns, ways of thinking, beliefs and filters that may be blocking success; NLP will help you to remove these blocks and truly be able to aim for and reach the success you desire in your life.

107. Develop Your Entrepreneurial Mindset

We meet a lot of people who want to be an entrepreneur but the majority either never embark upon that journey or they do and go back to employment within a few years.

Have you ever wondered what sets the successful entrepreneur apart from the wantrepreneur or unsuccessful entrepreneur? We know that the success ratio is about 20% of the product or service you are offering and 80% mindset.

NLP will help you to identify your own mindset, plus you will pick up tools that will help you to model other successful entrepreneurs to find out what they are doing that works. Once you can know the ingredients of the successful entrepreneurial mindset, you can then use your NLP skills to alter beliefs, change values, and update your unconscious filters and behaviours.

A wonderful thing that you will learn with NLP is a presupposition **if it is possible for someone else, it is possible for me**. And, because we have the skills to unpack the unconscious processes a person uses to reach a desired goal, you can then apply and adopt some of the successful strategies that someone else (or a few someone else's) use to be a successful entrepreneur.

108. Love Your Work

Not long ago, there was a gentleman in our NLP course in Singapore who had been doing the same job for 37 years, and he had loathed his job for 36 of those years. While talking to him, he couldn't think of anything else beneficial to his job other than the paycheque he received.

Unfortunately, he stayed in this job for so long because of the financial reward. It allowed him to take care of his family, provide a lifestyle he desired and pay for the things he and they desired. However, he had to work so much, for so long, and so hard that he barely had time to enjoy the very things the money was giving him.

He relished the weekends from Friday afternoon until Sunday evening. Starting after work on Friday his mood would improve, he would become more positive, powerful and creative. It was during the weekends (or when on holiday) that he would dream of his future and possibilities and hope. Then, Sunday evening would roll around and his mood would change, his behaviours would change and he would go into *work mode*, which, from his description sounded a lot like angry-depression. During the week, he had no energy or time or desire to dream or be creative to work toward his real goals and desires.

Part of his desire to learn NLP was to figure out a way to create a new path; in fact, what made his heart sing is the idea of being an NLP Coach and building a Wellness Centre with other Coaches and Allied Health Practitioners. He did gain a roadmap to begin his journey to becoming a coach, but being practical, he knew that it would take a while before he could quit his well-paying job to change career paths. So, an interim goal became to enjoy his job again.

To do this, he first looked at his values of his current role—which he deemed now as a 'filler-job.' He identified that the financial reward was indeed important, but he also was doing a job he had skills for, that was helping others and working in a team. All things he had dismissed before. He also looked at his emotional states and collapsed anchors that moved him into negative sates, and created new anchors that helped to access positive and resourceful states.

As long as a role is fulfilling your values and a positive or resourceful emotional state is being accessed, then you can fall in love with any job, role, situation, person, place or thing. NLP helped this gentleman to look forward to going to his filler-job—and he no longer loathed the work or the people or the concept. He knew it was just temporary. Because of this mood and energy shift, during the week his is studying, practicing and planning for his Coaching Business to take off at the end of the year.

Your mind is amazing – and we are creatures of habit. Habits are fairly easy to create—which can be a good and bad thing When you can get your mindset right, then you can love the work you do and do it well!

109. Identify What is Important to You in Business or a Career

If we asked you to write down 3-5 things that are important to you in your career, job or business, what would you write? In fact, if you had the opportunity, do that now. Make these one to three-word type phrases, like *make a difference, creativity, teamwork.*

In NLP, when we ask this question, "What is important to you about ___?" The question we are really asking is **what are your values**. Values, from an NLP perspective are what ultimately drives us; we are drawn toward or away from our values and they tend to be the drivers for our success.

When you can identify what is important to you in your career, job or business, then you have more ammunition to create success and happiness in your life. What you will learn with NLP is that when even one value on your list of 3-5 values is not being met, there is going to be a sense of unhappiness or discontentment or incongruence. For there to be a sense of fulfilment, success and genuine congruence, all your values must be met.

With NLP, you will learn how to change behaviours and beliefs that are attached to your values to help you get those values met. You will also learn how to change your values if they are outdated, redundant or not working for you. And, because it is our values which create drive within us, you can use your values to drive more motivation and success in your direction.

110. Model Others

Do you know anyone else who does something that you admire or something you would like to do? It might be their presentation skills, or confidence, or their ability to handle conflict well or to let things go. If you could gain some skills from someone else, what would you want to develop?

NLP was founded and is based on **modelling**. Modelling is the ability to identify the external behaviours and internal mindset that someone uses to achieve a result. When you model someone, you can learn from them and take on some of their perception, beliefs, mindset, unconscious filters, behaviours and more—but you only need to adopt what fits for you.

For example, a few years ago, we modelled a successful Coach who had a very successful and busy coaching practice. We wanted to model some of what he was doing so we could teach it to others, but there was something we didn't want to model—his ego and arrogance. Luckily, NLP will help you to identify the ingredients a person uses to reach success and helps you to create your own unique recipe.

Once you learn NLP and have the skills of modelling, we will invite you to keep your eyes open for people who you can model—they are all around you. And, a benefit for looking for what you want to model in others is that this will set you in growth mode and help you look for the best in others!

111. Developing Coaching Skills

If you are a manager, leader, owner, sales professional or anyone who leads, influences or motivates others, then developing coaching skills could be an imperative skill you should pick up from NLP.

The NLP Communication Model that you will learn is a key factor in your coaching skills – it will help you to understand why people are different from each other and require individual coaching styles. These days, coaching in the workplace is not a formal, sit-down performance-based process; it is an ongoing conversation which continually up-skills, checks-in and upgrades competency. A manager who does not have sound coaching skills cannot effectively lead individuals or teams to success; they can merely manage tasks and deadlines.

Coaching comes in many different forms, and you will gain a day-to-day capability of understanding the people around you and using their strengths and overcoming weaknesses to excel past personal and professional goals from NLP. If you want to be the best leader you can be, developing your coaching skills further will not only set your team up for more success, but you will also be fostering growth in others that will set you far apart from your colleagues.

112. Improve Your Productivity

Do you know your psychological make-up for when you are at your most productive? That might be workplace productivity or in any aspect of life. The most likely answer is no because most people are not aware of what makes them productive and what holds them back.

However, with NLP training, you will be able to identify what patterns of emotions, behaviours, thoughts and beliefs propel you forward. Additionally, you will identify anything that might be standing in your way from being as productive as you desire.

Applying the NLP tools, you will have the ability to change or transform any patterns you desire which might be holding you back, while at the same time supercharging what you normally and unconsciously do when you are in a productive state.

Can you imagine being able to tap-into your productivity at will? Not only will you understand what makes you tick, but you can also set up a variety of anchors, or triggers which will purposefully assist you to neurologically access your own personal state of productivity. In NLP, there is a presupposition, or assumption about human conditioning that states *you are in charge of your mind, therefore your results*. With NLP, you will learn how to take and maintain that charge of your mind.

113. Improve Workplace Productivity

The personal benefits of NLP are well known; you can tap into your own state of productivity and increase your output. And, as a leader or manager, you also have the ability to influence the productivity of others within your workplace.

The majority of a person's efficiency is the outcome of unconscious patterns, anchors, habits and beliefs. With the skills of NLP, you will be able to identify what the triggers are for your teammates, colleagues and employees that either motivate or demotivate them.

With this knowledge, you will be able to customise strategies for each person you work with to improve their productivity, create various tactics which will help your teammates to feed from the productivity of each other, and build a common sense of group rapport, cohesiveness and commitment to the team, business and overall common goals.

If you identify something in the workplace that demotivates an individual or your team, you can do something about that. We recently consulted for a company that had a KPI for their sales team that was outdated and demotivating for most of the team members. It was easy enough to change this criterion to something more motivational. If you identified that only one or a few people were negatively impacted, you could use your NLP skills to reframe, change or uncover the true meaning behind the lack of motivation for that person.

When a team or workplace is working in harmony, it becomes largely self-correcting. The overall productivity increases and the team begins to hold each other and themselves accountable to a new set of standards and initiatives. By understanding each person within a team through different models of NLP, you will be able to not only create more workplace productivity, you will be able to replicate that success in other teams.

114. Improve Your Confidence

Do you feel that your confidence level in the workplace is as high as outside of work? Interestingly, many people tell us they feel like an imposter or a fake at work because they aren't quite sure of their skills, attitudes and competencies compared to others.

If you are prone to comparisons, internal or external, you may need to boost your confidence levels at work. Internal comparisons would be a thought about where you think you *should be* compared to your past self-expectations, while external comparisons would be a direct comparison with yourself and someone else. Either of these elements could lower a person's confidence if they don't feel up to par with their comparisons.

Luckily, learning NLP will help you to turn any comparisons around to a learning aid which can boost your desire to improve, thus improving confidence. Additionally, you will be able to identify your own personal drivers for confidence and build a more resourceful confidence in any aspect of business. This might mean increasing your confidence to speak up in meetings, to ask for a sale, to speak in front of a group or even to take your own initiative to produce a change.

Many of the NLP concepts are based on modelling excellence, and this would include boosting your own confidence.

115. Boost Your Co-Workers' Confidence

Too many times we have felt a depressed workplace attempt to be productive and stimulating. A depressed workplace is one that does not foster growth, confidence or positive change; instead, it promotes fear, quantity-over-quality and self-doubt. Any team or workplace with a depressed stance is not one that will consistently achieve.

From a framework of NLP, you will be able to inspire your co-workers, teammates and subordinates to foster a growth-mindset which in turn will transform into self-belief, creative thinking and on-the-job confidence. By using NLP tools such as the meta-model, meta programs, Disney planning strategy plus creating a useful feedback loop, your teams' confidence will thrive and continue to produce remarkable results for your clients, teams and ultimately the company's bottom-line.

116. Learn to Manage Up

Have you ever been intimidated by your superiors in the workplace? It's quite common—especially if you have an affinity for being a perfectionist, have a fear of failure, if you don't quite have enough self-worth or if you were intimidated by an adult as a child.

The emotions, feelings and behaviours we have now as adults are largely driven by our experience. Our mind, however, is very malleable. With NLP, not only will you be able to address any interference that may be coming up, but you'll also gain a wealth of communication skills and tools that will help you to be more influential and communicate with anyone elegantly—at their level.

You will be learning simple mind tools including changing submodalities to change how your mind codes a thought, rapport skills to trigger the mirror neurons of anyone else, perceptual positions to be able to look and learn through someone else's perspective, neurological levels to ascertain different meanings, beliefs, behaviours and identities that people have, anchors to be able to trigger any state or feeling you want—when you want it—and state management that will allow you to be in the best state you desire for the situation at hand.

With your NLP skills, not only will you be able to lead your peers and employees, but you will also be that person everyone looks at with awe, someone who can communicate, lead, inspire and manage their superiors as well.

117. Be More Assertive

There used to be a trend of people attending assertiveness training. Most often, these people were shy, timid and unsure of themselves. They would learn a variety of skills to use, go back into their lives and continue to be shy, timid and unsure of themselves.

NLP doesn't teach tricks or tools to use in the moment; what you will gain from NLP is not just a conscious ability to do something different, but more importantly, a neurological mindset that is wired to new behaviours in different situations.

The main reason a person would need to increase their assertiveness skills is if they have a set of beliefs that do not allow for assertiveness as a reactionary trait. These beliefs lead to various behaviours, habits, emotions and skills which ultimately can be changed at the unconscious level.

By understanding the unconscious beliefs and programs of a person, you will be able to identify what type of communication is best for delivery, as well as a variety of NLP exercises that will clarify or resolve any interference to being assertive in the first place.

118. Handle Conflict Easier

Do you know that some people think that conflict is a natural part of life? They may not exactly *like* conflict, but they handle it better because of this belief. And equally, there are many people who would do anything humanly possible to avoid conflict because it is uncomfortable and often means someone is going to get hurt.

One of the factors that you will understand from NLP is the concept of meta programs, or unconscious filters that make sense of our world. One such meta program explains easily how some people handle conflict better than others; it is a filter that tells us how people make a decision or judgement.

Some people make decisions more theoretically and logically—these people fall into a category of *thinking.* They will dissociate from feelings if there is an emotional decision to be made and they will come to a conclusion based on the facts as they see it. You'll also notice that a person in a thinking mode may be quite blunt or direct – not taking into consideration how others will respond to them.

On the other side, we have a person who automatically associates to the feelings of others when making a decision—and they dislike any type of conflict, especially if someone may be hurt in any way. These people fall into a category of *feeling.* They will often over analyse how they will say something because they believe others also will want to avoid conflict.

When you learn about rapport, one thing you will learn is that when you are able to match or mirror some aspects of another person, you will be able to enter into a bond of rapport. One such aspect you can match is if someone is communicating in a thinking or feeling manner.

In order to better handle conflict, you will have access to great NLP tools including perceptual positions to be able to dissociate from an experience and step into a more logical and non-emotional perspective. Once again, we are reminded of an NLP presupposition that tells us *you are in charge of your mind, therefore your results.*

119. Understand Others Better

In the workplace, and beyond you will find people who are similar to you, and also different from you. Often, we find those that with those who are similar to us, we have a more natural flow of rapport with; after all, we tend to like people who are like us. This natural rapport helps us to more easily understand someone because we have a feeling that we know where they are coming from. But, that might not always be true. This type of rapport might actually mean we are assuming or mind-reading more because of our similarities.

The NLP communication model tells us that at every given moment, approximately 2,000,000 bits of information are coming into our unconscious awareness—yet we have only the ability to accept or compute 134 of those bits. Each of us chooses our own personally-selected 134 bits in a nano-second. This filtering is conducted in mere moments by our internal filtering process. That is, your unconscious filters store all of your memories, your beliefs, behaviours, habits, emotions, skills, competencies, dreams, and so much more than make you the special imprint of you.

Through a variety of NLP tools, including rapport, sensory acuity, meta-model questioning skills, meta-model and perceptual positions, you will learn how simple it is to truly understand someone.

There is a saying: "You cannot not communicate." As an NLP trained professional, you'll be able to see what isn't being said, hear with your five senses and really learn to better recognise and appreciate the differences that make each of us unique.

Improving Your Health with NLP

"You've only got one mind and one body in this lifetime, treat it with the respect, integrity and sense of awe that it deserves. You are responsible for that."

Laureli Blyth

120. Understand the Mind/Body Connection

One of NLP's presuppositions states that the mind and body are connected and therefore affect each other. Now suppose you realize this, but tend not to pay attention to it. When you feel hungry, you eat, when you have a headache, you might take an aspirin.

What if you learned to listen to your body and to find out what it is wanting you to pay attention to? Imagine your headache is the only way your mind can get you to shut off. You get the benefits of down-time but in a painful way. When you know the body communicates constantly, you can listen in a way you hadn't before.

NLP has amazing processes to get in touch with your own mind/body connection. It's one of the most important things you can do for yourself.

121. Improve Your Mental Health

Anxiety, depression, fears, addictions, instability; these mental health issues (and more) are created by a chemical reaction in your body, which is triggered by a conscious or unconscious pattern. Generally, anything regarding mental health can be helped by NLP.

A person's mental healthiness is formed greatly during childhood and adolescent years, and as we progress through life, various environmental factors impact us, too. I'm sure you've heard the saying, "It's not what happens to you but how you react to it that matters." Largely how you react is unconscious conditioning, which releases chemicals into your system, thereby creating a response.

Most people are not consciously aware of what their triggers are; it could be a smell, a thought, a colour, a sound—anything! And, there are somewhere around 2,000,000 bits of information coming into our awareness at any given moment, so it is unlikely that you would always be able to pinpoint what specifically is triggering an un-resourceful state or emotion.

A great thing about NLP, as you will learn, is that we don't need to know what the triggers are and we don't need to know what chemicals are being released. What we do need to know is what the emotional feeling is, and how you would rather unconsciously react instead.

With the tools of NLP, you will better understand the various patterns you experience of emotions and behaviours. Additionally, you will learn how to recognise, communicate with, and transform un-resourceful patterns of thought, emotion, behaviour, and beliefs. Using simple strategies, NLP will help you to take charge of your mental health to create a more healthy, robust, and resilient mindset.

122. Improve Your Physical Health

Do you realise that your mind and body are connected, and affect each other? Do you also realise that it is the unconscious part of your mind that is responsible for every bodily function you have? This includes the beating of your heart, digestion of food, body temperature regulation, chemical and hormone production, even your hunger pangs and blinking of your eyes.

Most people take for granted that the body is always doing what it is supposed to do without giving it much thought (unless it is not functioning or doing what they want). When there is an issue, people often look outside of themselves for answers and if their body does not co-operate, they blame it. We often meet people who have physical health issues that they have gone to see doctors, specialists, acupuncturists, physiotherapists, osteopaths, and more, and often the external treatment doesn't work because inside factors (psychological) are creating the issues.

NLP is well-known for its benefits in health and healing. In fact, NLP has many methodologies and tools that get your mind and body communicating so they know what each one wants and needs, and how to go about achieving this. For example, if you knew that your migraines are actually trying to tell you that you need to express yourself more, wouldn't that be a wonderful piece of information? Or, if your stomach ache or anxiety was your body's way of communicating its desire for you to change how you handle stress, could you use that information?

NLP will provide you with tools to understand what your unconscious (or automatic self) is doing and what it is programmed to do. Through a variety of NLP tools, you'll be able to align your beliefs, change behaviours, communicate with symptoms, and work directly with your chemical and hormone production to ensure optimal levels of production, while creating and maintaining neurological pathways that will keep you in beneficial health.

Learning and using NLP will give you the ability to manage your conscious thoughts and behaviours. As you learn how to communicate and manage your mind, you then improve your physical health in ways that will be long-lasting with beneficial effects.

123. Improve Your Emotional Health

Have you ever felt out of control of your emotions? Perhaps you go through experiences where you are angry, sad, frustrated, jealous, or even high emotions where it is hard to come down and relax. Sometimes it may feel like you are on an emotional rollercoaster with no end in sight.

Luckily, NLP contains some amazing and simple tools that will put you back in the driver's seat of your emotional health.

First, you will identify the patterns and meta-states (states or emotions beyond your emotions) that make up your current emotional patterns. For example, we recently worked with a gentleman who came for NLP Coaching to help him with rage and anger. His anger was exceptionally uncontrollable when he felt out of control of his situation, which, in his corporate life was most of the time. Through a variety of questions, we were able to uncover that the meta-states that made up his anger were fear and a lack of confidence.

Once you can un-pack an emotional state, you will then be able to apply some of the NLP techniques you will learn. Some NLP techniques will be used to access and build resources, like confidence, safety, self-worth, love, etc., and other techniques are used to clear interferences like fear, anger, stuckness, depression, etc.

Just because you have had a certain emotional reaction for most of your life doesn't mean you can't take charge of your emotional health and live a healthy, balanced emotional life.

124. Improve Your Spiritual Health

So, what does NLP have to do with spiritual health? Nothing, and yet everything. From a purely scientific perspective, spirit is outside and separate to a person. However, from our own perspective and point of view, humans are much more than just a mind and body; we are also spirit.

This doesn't necessarily mean God, angels, spirits or anything esoteric; however, depending on your beliefs, it might! For us, the spirituality of NLP encapsulates everything that is outside of 'proof.' This might include energy, intuition, dreams, knowingness, the collective universal consciousness, and yes, some of the esoteric elements.

If you've ever studied any energetic healing like reiki, psychometry, quantum theory, or even the law of attraction, you will already understand this aspect of spirituality.

Everyone has had an experience where you walk into a room where a heated argument has just occurred. You can *feel* that energy, can't you? That energy is simply matter. And we store this matter or energy inside and outside of ourselves. Sometimes, people have an energetic block that stops them from moving forward, continually provides examples of self-sabotage, and draws towards them what they *don't want* in life.

NLP contains a variety of tools that will help you to clear energetic blocks, create outlets to release negative energy, tap into positive resources, and create a spiritual flow to attract more of what you want in your life.

125. Communicate with the Unconscious Mind

Most of the things you do in your life are directed by what is in your unconscious mind. Communicating with the unconscious mind is something we do without realizing we are doing so. And as Carl Jung said," Until you make your unconscious mind consciously aware things will happen and you will call it fate."

Imagine having a way to communicate with your dear unconscious mind so you can direct your thoughts from the inside out. For instance, when you tell yourself you will do something and then find you don't follow through, like giving up a habit or sticking to a diet or exercise regime. You may have two different internal programs going on. One that says. 'yes to this,' and the other that says, "no," or, "that won't work," or, "we did that before and it doesn't work."

NLP teaches us how to communicate with the unconscious mind and how to program it so it serves us rather than us serving any unproductive programming.

126. Reset Metabolism

You've heard it before and we'll say it again: the mind and body are connected and therefore affect each other.

And the body can be a fickle thing! It runs on a program of health and can be swayed easily by beliefs, input (diet), and output (exercise). NLP can assist greatly with the belief parts of health. In fact, one belief we often work with is, "as I get older my metabolism slows down." Do you have this belief? If so, according to whom?

If it's not a universal truth (the sun will come up tomorrow, there are fish in the ocean, etc.), then it isn't a belief that exists for everyone. Do you know of anyone who is still fit, healthy and can eat whatever they want without a thought to their metabolism? What if metabolism were less of an age thing and more of a mind thing? Would you choose to do something about it?

Luckily, NLP has a few tools that will help for this! Namely, a process called **Communicating with Symptoms**, **Unconscious Pattern Change**, and **Neuro Repair Change** are all tools that you will learn with NLP that can help you to reset your metabolism, creating more energy, vibrancy, and a smaller waistline for you all at the same time.

127. Realign your Blueprint of Health

Do you realise that your unconscious mind contains a blueprint of you in perfect condition, body, mind, and spirit? And did you realise that you actually have the ability to tap into that blueprint and reboot your health back to its original state?

It has been said that disease is simply dis-ease of the mind/body connection. And, with NLP, we know and understand that the mind and body are connected, and therefore affect each other. Any illness, disease, pain, discomfort, or ailment most likely starts in the mind and manifests itself in the body to communicate its needs. However, most of the time we get too focused on whatever is going on in our world we forget to listen to our bodies.

Our cells are immensely flexible with a type of neuroplasticity that scientists are only now wrapping their heads around. While NLP cannot and will not profess to be a cure for anything, it can and will continue to assist people in creating healthy lives. We have seen tumours disappear, weight lost, memories regained, chronic illnesses evaporate, auto-immune deficiencies eliminated, and health re-established.

Using NLP, you will learn simple tools that will help you to communicate with your symptoms, rewire your neurology, balance your biochemistry, and realign your health with the blueprint you carry around in your cells.

128. Become More Aware of What is Going on with You

Have you ever had a backache, sniffle, pain in the neck, upset stomach, or niggling doubt of something that you just brushed off as normal yet mildly annoying? We all do that from time to time.

But, what if the sensations that you have in your body—including aches and pains—were a way for your body to communicate something to you? Think of it as a light knock on the door. If your mind were trying to communicate something to you, would you be able to dismiss it so quickly?

This is one of the ways that the body/mind connection works. If your body had a voice, we have no doubt that it would talking to you all the time; but since it doesn't have an auditory voice, it has created a physical one. In NLP, we look at everything having a positive intention, even pains, urges, emotions, diseases, and more.

When you learn NLP, you'll learn how to speak your own language, that is, the language of your body. You will become more mindful of what your "normal" truly is; and anything outside of your normal is something you can begin to communicate with. In fact, NLP has a specific technique called **Communicating with Symptom**s that will help you to do just this.

A recent example is a gentleman who completed our NLP Level 1 training. He had been experiencing lower back pain for the past 3 or so years. He had concluded that the back pain was caused by bad posture. He had even gone to the length of purchasing a lower back support which kept his spine straight. However, it wasn't taking away the pain. In the class, he communicated with the back pain and he began to understand that his pain was communicating the desire of his unconscious mind to be stronger with his in-laws, people who he often lost his strength with and bowed down to what they wanted.

The unconscious mind is very symbolic; he told us that what he observed as a movie in his mind about standing tall wasn't about posture. The feelings that came with standing tall included strength, using his voice, standing up for himself and taking back control. When asked who he needs this type of strength with, he thought for a moment and realised it was his in-laws. We then used a variety of other tools to help him to stand in his strength. Interestingly, once he came to this understanding, the pain began to subside, and last we checked with him, the pain was gone completely and he is still maintaining his strength and personal control with his in-laws.

When you are more aware of what is going on in your mind and body, you can then become more understanding of what is going on for you. This might be a physical pain, an emotion, a behaviour, or even a craving or urge. If you are procrastinating about something, there is a good chance your unconscious mind need or wants something before you begin. If you are craving chocolate, it might not be the chocolate but something else your unconscious mind needs and desires.

A great assumption about NLP is that you are in charge of your mind and therefore your results. When you are more aware about what is going on for you, you are one step closer to being fully in charge of your mind.

129. Create a Sense of Internal Safety

The base of Maslow's Hierarchy of Needs is made up of what he considers our human basic needs: the physiological needs like water, food, warmth, and rest and our security needs. Without these basic needs being met, there will be a sense of disorder to our lives. We may have our physiological needs met, but if innately we do not feel safe, we can never be truly free to express ourselves, be vulnerable, be loved, or as Maslow puts it, attain self-actualisation.

So, I pose a simple question for you that may or may not have simple ramifications.

Are you safe?

When we meet people who have fears, phobias, anxiety, worry, depression, self-doubt, or a need for control, we often find a deep-rooted lack of safety. Even when the person is physically safe in their present moment, the unconscious mind is working overtime to protect, secure, and keep the person safe.

This safety mechanism occurs in many ways. The most common are excess physical weight, anxiety, fears, and hypervigilance when no vigilance is needed.

Parents who are over-protective are often missing internal safety themselves. Unfortunately, our children are continually learning from us, so while we may be keeping our children safe, we are teaching them to be over-protective of themselves and others. Ultimately, we cultivate the cycle to be stronger and repeated over time.

If safety is a basic need, where does it come from and where does it go?

Let's look at our ancestors, all the way back from caveman days to just a few generations ago. My guess is that they were alert much of their lives, looking out for wild animals, neighbouring villages, hostile allies, and keeping their families, goods, and properties safe. An ongoing need to be aware of immediate dangers would be enough to trigger our innate fight or flight response, constantly turning on our amygdala and engaging our adrenaline and cortisol levels to be 'on guard.'

Now, for most of us, we don't have immediate danger within our present situation. However, we have the capacity and function to choose fight or flight at any moment. Our brain is wired to seek safety first and ask questions last.

If you have been in situations in the past where your physical or emotional safety was under threat—even if only for a moment or a perceived moment—this could be enough to trigger and create a program of constantly seeking safety. Luckily, when you learn NLP, you will gain a variety of tools to reset your levels of safety and security, allowing your unconscious mind to relax and let you be safe without having to be alert all the time.

Can you imagine what it would be like to simply feel safe, knowing that there is no imminent danger? Most likely, your choices will expand, your security will increase, your confidence will boost, and you will be able to step into a sense of freedom and ease that you've only dreamed about. By clearing unconscious patterns and boosting resources with NLP, you will be able to have this life. Finally, and forever, safe.

130. Promote Quick Healing

The human body is truly remarkable. Without thinking, alarms, timers, or reminders, our unconscious mind is working behind the scenes to keep our body fresh. In fact, did you know that your body is continually regenerating itself? It is. The outer layer of your skin replaces itself every 35 days (and you thought it was just *dust* hanging around your house!). Your body produces a new liver every six weeks. Your stomach lining is replaced every four days, and stomach cells that comes into contact with food are replaced every five minutes. Every three months your skeleton structure is regenerated, and your entire brain is replaced every two months. And, every five to seven years, every atom is replaced. The only thing that remains is your neurology, but the pathways your neurons fire on are also replaced.

All of this happens without your conscious involvement, throughout the day, and as you sleep at night.

So, if all of this happens without your conscious involvement, what could you imagine might occur if you were involved in some of your health and healing?

Say for example, if you badly burned your hand. Do you think you could use your mind to speed up the healing process? We do.

With NLP, you can affect all aspects of your life. Through a variety of visualisation type of techniques, you will learn how to alter your chemical production, healing centres, and health promotion within your body. Your body will continue to regenerate itself in the same way it always does, but with the ability to kick start some key neuro transmitters, you can promote health and healing more quickly and efficiently than just leaving your body to do it on auto-pilot.

Additionally, you can use NLP to supercharge your healing by adding additional resources into your awareness and system. For example, if a person is deficient in calcium, their bones and skeleton may rejuvenate weaker each time. Using the mind as a springboard, you will learn to increase the self-production of the resources needed to create strong bones. Of course, an increase in dietary calcium wouldn't hurt! But, with NLP you can speed up the application and regrowth of strong healthy bones.

The more neuroscience is getting to understand the mind/body connection it is becoming clearer and clearer how much control we truly do have over our own body and health. This is something that NLP has known for decades.

131. Overcome Depression

Depression for too many people has become an unfortunate way of life. More and more people are suffering with depression, not knowing how to get out from under the heavy dark cloud of despair. Unfortunately, the medical system isn't doing much to help other than doling out prescriptions for antidepressants, and for the many people who don't want to be introduced to man-made chemicals, their depression stays untreated.

Speaking of pharmaceuticals, did you know that there is not a test of any kind that marks the need for antidepressants? None.

When a person is depressed, there is an imbalance of chemicals and neurotransmitters being produced, namely serotonin, dopamine, and norepinephrine. If the brain is creating a deficient amount of chemicals naturally, antidepressants may help restore a balance to a person's mood, allowing them to feel whole again.

However, if the cause is situational, that is, the loss of a job, change of relationship, death of a loved one, etc., the chemical imbalance is most likely not going to be fixed by antidepressants. We often find that when a person is unnecessarily on antidepressants, they describe a feeling like walking in a fog or being disconnected to life. The induced chemicals create more of a flat-line of emotions: no highs and no lows.

So, if drugs are not the answer, what is?

Well, NLP is a great choice for working with and overcoming depression. You see, with NLP, you will be able to reboot the nervous system in a way that can kick-start the appropriate levels of chemical release, thus balancing the chemicals naturally. Additionally, if the depression is situational, NLP will help you to re-evaluate past experiences to let go of the old emotions, store the learnings to be more empowered, and step into new states and emotions.

Even if the cause of the depression is unknown, and if you haven't *always* been depressed, learning NLP will provide you with the skills to unpack the unconscious patters and make changes at a deep level which will automatically influence the creation of chemicals.

Unlike many other forms of psychotherapy, NLP pays specific attention to a person's desired state. Instead of simply understanding your depression, where it comes from, and providing some coping strategies to live with it, NLP takes it a step further by asking, "what do you want instead?"

If a person has been living with chronic depression, being able to even ascertain a desired state may take a while. And that's okay, because depression—the imbalance of chemicals and neurotransmitters—can be amended by getting to know the structure of the depression and using the unconscious mind to make a change for the better.

You will also develop NLP skills to help other people change their programming and overcome their depression, too.

132. Overcome Anxiety

One of our favourite definitions of anxiety and worry is: *the hallucination of what might possibly go wrong in the future.*

Most of the most successful people in the world think about what pitfalls may lay ahead, but they don't dwell on them; instead, they plan for them appropriately.

Anxiety, true anxiety, has chemicals involved in it, and anxiety is rampant in today's world. Chemically, it is understood that anxiety is created by too much adrenaline and noradrenaline, not enough serotonin and GABA (gamma-aminobutyric acid), which puts the body into a state of hyper-alertness, awaiting the fight or flight mechanism to kick in.

We wonder however, which comes first? The imbalance of chemicals or unconscious programming that triggers the imbalance of chemical production?

From an NLP perspective, we can look at anxiety in a couple of ways. The first is simply biochemical: we can use the unconscious mind to trigger the creation and secretion of chemicals in the right balance. And secondly, we can reprogram the unconscious mind so that anxiety isn't triggered in the first place.

From investigation with our clients and students, we can put the rise down to three things: 1) the desire for instant gratification, 2) more comparisons of where people think they should be in life, and 3) the fear of being judged. The second and third elements help to explain why social anxiety is on the rise.

When you learn NLP, you will be learning how to manage your state, which will help you on a moment-to-moment basis to control your thoughts, feelings, and actions. But anxiety usually goes deeper than that. You will also learn how to identify unconscious patterns and programming that trigger anxiety in the first place, and you will find out how to change this programming to create a balanced emotional and chemical state, therefore reducing anxiety.

But reducing or completely getting rid of anxiety often isn't enough. Along with your NLP tools, you will also learn how to access and build personal resources such as self-belief, confidence, self-worth, positive regard, strength, and resilience. We've found that these are key resources that are often not present when someone is overcome with anxiety.

With NLP, you can be more aware of the emotions you have and take proactive steps to create a state that is more beneficial to you in any moment. Imagine that, living anxiety free. Finally.

133. Stepping into Wholeness

Have you ever experienced a feeling like there was a battle going on in your life? Perhaps it's like you are being *pulled* in different directions? Or you heart says one thing, but your brain says another? Maybe you really want to follow your dreams, but something stops you?

In NLP, we call these components of our internal battles **parts**. Simply put, different **parts** of ourselves in conflict with each other.

Various studies of the mind have found that when we have one direction and one focus, we function more effectively. We tend to be happier, more motivated, more productive, and more aligned with our goals and ourselves.

Great news! NLP has quite a few techniques which focus on creating wholeness. **Parts Integration** is one such classic technique that will help you to identify the incongruent parts and help them to find common ground in working together, even unifying for your wholeness. **Six Step Reframe** will help you to negotiate between the parts to settle conflict. **Neurological Levels Alignment** will assist you to align your environment, behaviours, capabilities, beliefs and values, identity, and greater whole for more wholeness. **Multiple Brain Alignment** will allow your head, heart, and gut to function in alignment with each other.

When you can bring more wholeness into your life and into your awareness, it is easier to make decisions, find your state of flow, and increase your happiness and your overall well-being.

What parts do you have that are out of alignment?

134. Release Negativity

Some people tend to be more naturally "glass is half empty" type; what makes them that way? And do they *have* to be that way?

The answer to the first is quite simple. Historical programming has created a belief that triggers the behaviours of negativity and negative thinking. In fact, the reason(s) why we do anything can be tracked back to beliefs that we created at some point in our lives.

The answer to the second question is also simple. If a person wants to release their negativity, NLP contains many tools that will help us get to the root cause of the belief structure and realign their beliefs, behaviours, and thoughts with a more positive or balanced outlook on life. However, not everyone wants to release negativity.

Yes, this is true. Not long ago we met a gentleman who had a metaphorical chip on his shoulder. He was the friend of a colleague, not a client or student, but we could talk about his negativity and negative view on the world. He explained that he hadn't always been so negative, but the world had dealt him a bad hand of cards and one way he had figured out to manage what life gave him was to be on-guard all the time. He looked for problems, not results. He mismatched his friend, and found their pitfalls. He dwelled on worst case scenario and planned to fail, yet rarely failed.

He wasn't what I would consider happy, but he was strangely content. I say strangely, because it was somewhat foreign to me. But through NLP, you will learn to respect others' models of the world. For him, his negativity created a safety mechanism, one that was at that moment working for him.

If he had wanted to, or if he chooses to make a change in the future, NLP could help him to release his negativity. But first, we would need to use NLP to build resources for safety so he could release the safety mechanism that negativity has created for him. We could then address the beliefs, values, behaviours, and other unconscious patterns connected to this pattern so he could fully release negativity.

If you have a cloud of negativity that you live with, you have a choice. Once it is no longer serving its purpose, then perhaps you can choose to apply your NLP techniques to releasing negativing, and stepping into more positivity and more balance in life.

135. Become More Positive

A person's viewpoint of positive optimism or more negative-based thinking is often a product of unconscious programming. Our programming is made generally of our past experiences, which develops into beliefs, emotions, behaviours, habits, and aspects of our identity.

If one of your goals is to create a more positive outlook on the world, yourself, or an aspect of life, NLP can help with that!

When you use the techniques and strategies of NLP, it will help to sort through your own mind and manage your thoughts. When you are more positive, you can be more forward-thinking, more present, happier and fully congruent or aligned with where you are now, and where you are going.

Some of the benefits to being more positive include improving your health and overall well-being, finding more happiness, fun, and joy in the little things, less stress and anxiety, reduced depression, sadness, and lethargy, increase energy levels, and a boost creativity, confidence, and self-esteem.

If you find yourself in a rut of negativity about something specific or in general, applying the knowledge, methods, and skills of NLP could be your key to success. After all, creating a more positive outlook leads to enthusiasm, and we know that enthusiasm is contagious!

136. Remove Allergies

From an NLP standpoint, allergies are one way the unconscious mind communicates something to you and keeps you healthy and safe at the same time. However, what if you could understand what the mind was wanting to communicate to you? What if you could use your mind and body to overcome allergies?

One of our colleagues, NLP Trainer Bob Roberts, says, "Allergies have to do with the immune system getting out of control. Our unconscious mind has control over our immune system. As we know, when we're run down and stressed out, we're more likely to get a cold, because the stress has depressed our immune system defences. Logically, it follows that as NLP has techniques to connect with and influence our unconscious mind, then NLP techniques can also be a way to directly influence our immune system."

Your body may react in certain ways because of various beliefs, needs that are not being met, or impulses. Some allergies or intolerances are our bodies way of communicating a need to us; for some, it may be an emotional need, that when met will allow the allergy to go away, while other people may experience an allergy due to a certain belief.

For example, we recently worked with a woman who was allergic to gluten; she would have a specific reaction anytime she ate bread or anything with gluten. In order to not have these reactions, she had simply chosen to remove these food items from her diet. Using a variety of NLP techniques, we could pinpoint her association to bread (and all other gluten) to a childhood memory of her parents violently fighting while her older brother made all the siblings a sandwich. Once we cleared this old connection and recreated new pathways for gluten, she can once again enjoy sandwiches, pizza, cakes, and many other gluten favourites!

137. Create Resilience

Why do some people bounce back from trauma and other people crumble at the thought of it? This question always intrigued me, and I wrote my doctoral thesis about it.

Resilience is the ability to bounce back from difficult situations, to adapt well in the face of adversity, trauma, tragedy, and change. Being resilient does not make someone immune to difficulty or distress; it simply means that you will rebound more quickly and robustly. It isn't a quality that someone either has or not; it can be cultivated, built, and developed.

There are a few key factors or resources involved with the creation of resilience that can be built or enhanced with NLP. Namely: self-trust, a positive outcome, a positive outlook, and a connection with others.

In fact, when you learn NLP, you will have a toolbox of skills to help yourself and others become more resilient. You'll be able to clear any beliefs or unresourceful patterns that may hold people back from self-trust or a positive outlook, to create anchors to help people connect easier with others, and to access states of self-esteem to promote trust and self-reliance. The NLP well-formed outcome process helps to create a positive and clear outlook for the future and you can also help someone build more desire to be with others and foster a connective relationship.

Being able to be resilient can assist in so many situations, from workplace and relationship changes, to health issues and illness, the loss of loved ones, and even being able to accept criticism and feedback. It's also wonderful to know that resilience is a trait and resource that can be developed through your NLP skills. The next step from here is post-traumatic growth: becoming even stronger, more robust and not just the ability to bounce back, but bounce *forward*.

138. Work with Physical Illness

While NLP would never profess to cure illnesses, we know that there are so many illnesses, physical and mental, that have been transformed because of NLP.

The mind and body are connected and therefore affect each other. If there is a physical illness within the body, we can use the mind to begin the healing process.

Throughout the years, we have helped so many people with physical illness using NLP. To name a few things, we have helped people to transform chronic pain, hypothyroidism, carpal tunnel, endometriosis, cancer, digestive issues, high blood pressure, migraines, infertility, erectile dysfunction, public urination issues, low sex drive, chronic fatigue (ME), fibromyalgia, allergies, and so much more.

Sometimes, the symptoms of the illness go away all together, sometimes it is reduced, and sometimes nothing happens at all. When we are using NLP to work with physical illness, our aim at first is to create more understanding about what the body needs. You see, the way the body communicates to your conscious mind is through physical sensations, sometimes resulting in illness.

There are many NLP techniques aimed at creating better health and working with the symptoms of an illness to better understand and give it what it wants. When you learn NLP, you will be able to communicate with symptoms in this way that will give you more power about choices you're making, behaviours you have, and options before you.

139. Release Addictions

If you talk to someone with an addiction, they will be the first person to tell you how hard it is to change behaviours and release the addiction. This is because when most people try to break an addiction, they do so hoping willpower or mind diversion will work. Most of the time it does not. Or, they give up one addiction for another.

There are so many things that a person can be addicted to: alcohol, cigarettes, drugs, gambling, food, but there are others. These include addictions to people, phones, gaming, love, sex, chocolate, being needed, helping others, and so many other possibilities.

From experience of working with addictions for many years, willpower and diversion is not enough. Not by a longshot.

Ultimately, an addiction is the need or craving for something and the inability to give it up.

If someone tells me, "I just need willpower," I know right away that there is not a strong enough desire for change. Anything, and I mean anything, you strongly desire takes absolutely zero willpower. You just do it.

Let's look at addictions for a moment. When it comes to NLP, we see that every behaviour has a positive intention—even a secondary gain or a benefit for keeping a behaviour. For example, a person who smokes may have a positive intention of relaxing for those 5-10 minutes a few times a day. Or the alcoholic may desire a way to check out and be numb to life; if they were sober, they would have to face up to emotions, decisions, or feelings they don't want to address. The person who turns to chocolate in times of stress may not have the resources to say what they need to, so chocolate becomes a friend.

When you start looking at addictions through the lens of NLP, you will stop looking at the label of the addiction and start looking at the symptoms, positive intention, and secondary gain. You will then be able to tap into your toolbox of NLP skills to clear unresourceful patterns of emotion, belief, and behaviour while building and accessing resources that will make the change possible. And in the end, everyone is different.

Ultimately, the *reason* for anyone's addiction is individual to them. No two people have the same history, beliefs, programming, or behaviours, and to treat them as if there is a cookie-cutter approach to releasing the addiction is about as useful as relying on willpower.

It isn't until the unconscious patterns are fully addressed that a person will be able to easily and effortlessly release their addiction. Using NLP techniques to make changes to this programming, where there is a clear and desired goal, becomes easy and addictions can then be released without the need for willpower. It becomes want-power instead!

140. Release Trauma

The mind is an amazing machine: it has instant protection mechanisms that help keep us safe, and for the most part does a great job of doing so. However, sometimes in traumatic situations, be it a fight, an accident, or even war, our unconscious mind has trouble separating us from the past and it seems to get stuck in a perpetual traumatic state. This is ultimately what post-traumatic stress disorder (PTSD) is; our mind and body are emotionally stuck with an associated response to trauma, even if it isn't happening now.

In the mid-1970's, the founders of NLP, Richard Bandler and John Grinder, devised an NLP technique from an assortment of tools that came from Dr Milton Erickson's work with hypnosis and Fritz Perls work with Gestalt Therapy. This process is still taught at the NLP Practitioner level and is called the **Visual Kinaesthetic Dissociation Process.**

The basic premise for this process is to recreate a memory where one is separated from their feelings by being outside one's own body. Ultimately, they are watching themselves in a dissociated position flow through the old event to a point of safety and wholeness.

With NLP, you can assist yourself and others to release trauma, move on from the past, and disconnect from events that still affect them. This specific NLP tool is widely used to assist military veterans overcome PTSD and is the main NLP tool used in a study being conducted for the NLP Research and Recognition project with a current success rate of over 90%!

141. Transform Eating Disorders

I have a non-NLP trained friend who works as a counsellor at an in-patient eating disorder clinic. She is amazed at the out-patient success rates I have with my clients, only using NLP. Even though she has seen the proof of changes occurring, she still remains openly sceptic about my NLP approach. I still have hope that she'll see the light one day and come onto the NLP side and truly help people more efficiently. I do however, know that if the clinic were to use NLP, they wouldn't need the clinic anymore!

For years, I've been interested in eating disorders of all sorts. I find them challenging disorders to work with because of their complexity, but I find the people and treatment with NLP simple and beneficial.

You see, where traditional counselling and therapy will address the problem and attempt to change behaviours on a surface level, or delve into the depths of history to understand and transform it, NLP takes a different approach. NLP looks at a person's unconscious patterns of belief, thought, and emotion, and filters that lead to the behaviours of an eating disorder.

While the underlying reasons and root cause are different for each person, I have found a common theme or set of filters that people with eating disorders tend to use in life. Through questioning tools and various NLP techniques, we begin to address these filters, and then work with any underlying issues, memories, patterns, or emotions that may be causing the use of these filters.

These filters are: perfectionism, a pattern of all-or-nothing, a fear of failure or fear of success, and a need for control. Again, for each person, these filters will have been created for different reasons from different situations, but they exist in most all people. Some stem from abuse (sexual or otherwise), some from being abandoned in some way, some from not feeling worthy or good enough, and some from totally different reasons.

Once the filters have been addressed and changed using NLP, and the root cause has also been addressed, the need for the eating disorder is no longer present. We simply work on the behavioural habits that have transpired over time. I've found when working NLP and eating disorders that when a person is ready to make a change and is ready to address the root cause, the changes are quick, profound, and deeply beneficial.

I'm still hoping my friend who works at the eating disorder clinic will come around to my way of thinking sooner than later! There are so many lives that can be positively impacted through NLP.

142. Lose Weight

As NLP Coaches or Therapists, we are not nutritionists and we are not personal trainers. We do not give advice about food or exercise, but we are interested in both. We do not create a health regime or a plan of action to lose weight, but people seek our help to do just that—lose weight. And, with the use of NLP, most people are very successful at this endeavour!

It has been said that when it comes to losing weight, its 80% food and 20% exercise. We'd like to change those stats a little. We think its 30% psychology and mindset, 50% food, and 20% exercise. You see, the mindset of a person makes a tremendous difference on overall results, the amount of time it takes to lose weight, and the ability to keep it off.

And, while we are interested in what someone eats and how they move their body, our reasons for wanting to know these things are different than why a nutritionist or personal trainer might want to know. As an NLPer, you will want to know this information because a person's behaviours are the most important information you can find out. This is because a person's behaviours are directly correlated to a person's beliefs and values. And a person's beliefs and values answer the question, "Why." "Why can't I lose weight?" "Why do I eat when I'm stressed?" and "Why am I not motivated to go to the gym?" The answers are simple: because you have beliefs and values aligned with your current behaviours.

When you are trained in NLP, you will then have the tools to address, realign and transform these beliefs and values—therefore transforming behaviours and habits at the same time.

Everything happens first at an unconscious level; all our patterns of emotion, beliefs, and behaviours stem from this unconsciousness. Logic, reasoning, and logical thinking: the way most people try to figure out their behaviours are *not* unconscious. I've never met a person who could successfully logic themselves into long-term weight loss.

And, everyone is different. Not one person's 'why' is exactly like someone else's. And, most of the time, the beliefs we hold onto that create unwanted behaviours and habits have absolutely nothing to do with weight.

One of our favourite examples is about a young woman who desperately wanted to lose weight and had done *everything* to do this. Every fad, every program, every gym, every everything – and she *would* lose weight. Science doesn't lie: energy in, energy out. But she couldn't *keep* it off. We worked with a few NLP timeline processes that help us to track back a pattern to beliefs we have.

This woman went back in her unconscious memory to a movie of a young girl who was 2-3 years old. The girl was frightened and felt lost; she wanted to know, "what's going on" and the message she kept hearing from her parents (who interestingly were separating around this time) was, "you're too little, you can't handle it. When you are bigger, you can handle it." Now, the unconscious mind is very literal and it takes everything literally and personally. If her parents did reply with this message, ultimately, they would have meant, "you are too young, when you are older you will be able to handle this," but that isn't how her unconscious mind filtered it, is it?

No. Her unconscious mind filtered it based on 'too little' meaning in regards to size. After clearing this belief from the past, the woman started to identify all the times in her life when she was stress free and she could easily lose weight. However, if even a little stress came her way, she couldn't "handle it" and she would put on weight. Her unconscious mind had created a belief that she had to be "bigger" to handle things.

None of this had to do with food. But, it had everything to do with her pattern of losing weight. We used NLP to change that belief, change her behaviours around stress, give her new outlets to handle stressful situations, and she could lose weight. And, more importantly, *keep it off.*

With your NLP skills, you will be able to uncover beliefs in any area of life that might be holding you back from attaining your desired state. And if weight loss is a goal of yours, you'll be able to find your own beliefs that may get in your way and transform them so your behaviours align with your goals. With NLP, weight loss can be easy!

Maybe we'll change the stats to 50% psychology and mindset, 40% food, 10% exercise!

143. Quit Smoking

If you had 10 minutes every few hours, or even a few times a day, to relax, chill-out, disconnect, breathe deeply and take a break, why would anyone give that up? Most people wouldn't, unless it had a cigarette on the end of it. Yet, with all the knowledge available today about the negative effects of smoking, so many people still do it.

Addictions, habits and behaviours such as smoking are fairly easy to change with NLP. The trick is, we don't treat *smoking*; we treat the benefits you get from smoking and address the habit.

The unconscious mind is an interesting thing. It not only stores all our memories and emotions, but it also is tremendously easy to program and re-program. It works best with repetition and habits, which is why the act of smoking is so easy to create a habit of. This also means that it can be an easy habit to break, too.

But it's not just the habit; that's the easy part we can do with NLP. You will learn how to change the coding of your unconscious mind so we can begin to rewire how you think, feel, and act toward cigarettes and smoking. This also seems to change or re-route the nicotine in the brain, cutting off any cravings or symptoms of cravings. This in turn creates a halt in the behavioural habit.

The more important aspect of any addiction is looking at the *meaning and belief* that has been put on smoking. If smoking means 'taking a break,' or 'gathering my thoughts,' or 'disconnecting from life,' we use our NLP skills first identify how you want to achieve these things instead of smoking. If someone is about to lose their ability to relax a few times a day, do you really think they are going to quit smoking?

No.

As a Coach working with people to quit smoking, we identify a persons desired state. It's not just, "I want to quit smoking," but it's often more involved than that. We want to know what *life* is going to be like smoke-free. Then we will use our NLP techniques to change old beliefs, build resources, and create a mind frame-work to not only remove smoking from their unconscious awareness, but to ensure they don't miss out on any of the positive benefits smoking provided them in the first place.

144. Improve Your Happiness

Do you believe that you are in charge or your mind, your life and your emotions? What if you did believe that, and what if you were? Would that change your level of happiness?

Too often when we talk to people about happiness, we are told things like, "I'll be happy when," or, "I'm not happy because of," or, "X takes my happiness away." These statements take happiness out of a person's control and puts happiness as something external to achieve or strive for.

We're sure you know people who try to change their environment to create happiness; they change jobs, move out of state or country, or get into a new relationship. All to seek and find happiness. Is happiness really a commodity that you can *find*?

What if happiness were simply a state of mind. What if you didn't have to search for happiness, but you could choose it?

This is what NLP will help you to do.

You see, your definition of happiness is made up of everything you've done, learned, believed, observed, and identified with. In fact, in NLP we call that your **model of the world**. In NLP, we also have a few assumptions about life including everything has a positive intention and we are all doing the best with the resources we have available, and everyone is in charge of their own mind and therefore their beliefs.

Your beliefs about happiness and life are simply the current truths that you hold onto. Some people believe that happiness comes from outside. Taking a stem from positive psychology, NLP sees happiness simply as a state, not an identity.

A state is a mood or emotion; it is made up of two things: 1) the feelings you feel inside your body and 2) your physiology and body. When you change either of these aspects, your state starts to change.

When you start to use NLP to boost your happiness, you will start from the inside out. Not only will you begin to make a conscious effort to look up, smile, relax your shoulders, breathe deeply, and move around, but you will also use many of the NLP techniques to change your beliefs, definitions, and concepts around happiness.

If you have a 'reason' for your happiness not being as robust as you want it, you will have access to many techniques that will finally put those reasons to bed. After all, you are not your past. While your past may have shaped your now, you have choice about what happens next, how you process and react to the past.

With NLP, you can create more happiness in all aspects of your life. You might even choose one of our favourites: to be happy for no reason at all!

Using NLP with Others

"NLP contains so many useful tools, why would you keep them to yourself? Share them, use them, help make the world a better place by choosing to use your NLP skills with others."

Dr. Heidi Heron

145. Become an NLP Therapist

It used to be that people only sought the help of a therapist when they were referred by a doctor because something was wrong. It took months and months, even years and years to feel benefit of the therapy.

Times have changed, my friend, times have changed. With the development of brief-therapies, people are learning more about how the mind works and how tools like Neuro Linguistic Programming (NLP) can facilitate change at a rapid pace.

So, if you have a calling to a helping profession, but actually want to help others, then NLP is worth considering. Let me tell you more.

As an NLP Therapist, you will be able to assist people with a range of issues, including depression, anxiety, addictions, fears, lack of confidence, procrastination, negativity, lack of motivation, communication issues, and more. As you can see, NLP addresses similar topics to what a traditional counsellor or therapist might, but more breadth and in a much quicker timeframe.

NLP is the study of excellence, modelled after 3 prime therapists in the 1970's that all worked directly with the unconscious mind; this is the part of your mind that actually runs your body, emotions, reactions, and more! In fact, as an NLP Therapist, your job is to understand *how* the language of your clients' mind is created and how it triggers patterns and programs unconsciously. As an NLP Therapist, you are less interested in what the story of your client is and more interested in how the story evolved.

You'll identify where your client is and what they want by asking a variety of specialised questions aimed at uncovering what has been distorted, deleted, and generalised by the conscious mind. Through further questioning, you'll begin to understand what is holding your client back, or interfering with their progress. This might mean finding unresourceful habits, behaviours, patterns of thoughts, emotions, or actions. And, you'll identify what resources your client requires; for example, your client may need more confidence, self-belief, or a voice.

Then, once we understand all of that, you will then implement a variety of tools that you'll learn as an NLP Practitioner and Master Practitioner to clear and transform any interferences, while also accessing and building resources your client needs.

And the best thing? You will be working with your client's unconscious mind to make the changes. This bypasses the need for a pure talk-therapy formula and starts creating action and movement right away.

Generally, an NLP Therapist will work with a client in 6-12 one-hour sessions, staying well within the limits of traditional brief therapy, which is deemed as anything less than 20 hours.

No previous training is required to start your journey at becoming an NLP Therapist; generally, your study with NLP Worldwide will span about 12 months and then you can begin your full or part-time career as an NLP Therapist.

146. Become an NLP Coach

Not so long ago, when someone mentioned a Coach, people thought about sports. Then the introduction of Executive Coaches evolved and eventually Life Coaches. It is now a field on its own and more and more people are seeking the guidance of a Coach.

NLP, although originally modelled on psychotherapy, has the foundation for a strong and robust coaching modality. While some schools merely add in a few of the communication tools, NLP is the only tool we teach to our NLP Coaches.

You see, most traditional coaching schools teach a format that helps a Coachee to identify what they want and the steps necessary to get there; the Coach then provides motivation and accountability to the Coachee. Often, the Coaches are taught that if emotions or psychological barriers come up, they should refer the client on to a therapist.

NLP goes many steps above and beyond this. NLP is focused on the whole person, starting with their unconscious mind. It is the unconscious mind that truly drives a person to success.

First, NLP contains a Communication Model that outlines how a person filters information, skills to become more sensory aware of what your client is saying (and not saying), tools to build a supportive rapport, and questioning techniques to uncover what may be hidden from the conscious mind, including beliefs, emotions, and other barriers that may hold a person back.

Secondly, after using the communication skills of NLP as a Coach, you will then have an arsenal of tools available to you to create goals that are well-formed in idea, belief, emotion, structure, and execution; to help to build any resources, attitudes, attributes, or skills that are needed; and to help clear any interferes to success that may come up.

As a Coach, you can use your NLP skills in any type of Coaching situation: personal, life, executive, corporates team, group, sporting—you name it! Your NLP skills will give you the resources to assist your clients to obtain and even go beyond their goals. And, at the same time, the skills and resources you are helping them to access and build are transferable to every aspect of life.

Coaching sessions with NLP are very similar to traditional Coaching: you can work with people in individual sessions, or you can create packages. The most common package we see to achieve a goal is 3-6 months, but that could be expanded depending on the breadth of a goal or outcome.

To become an NLP Coach, there is no pre-requisite learning or experience needed. Our full NLP Coach Certification program takes approximately 12 months to complete and you will start working with clients well before then as you practice and refine your NLP Coaching skills.

147. Become a Better Parent

Who is a Coach to your children? When asked this, many parents name teachers or sporting coaches or tutors. And, while these answers technically are correct, they are missing out on their child's primary Coach.

Themselves.

If you are a parent, you are a Coach. If you have more than one child, you have to be a different kind of Coach to each of your children to meet their individual needs, style, and objectives.

As a parent, you are motivating, inspiring, encouraging, teaching, supporting, and challenging your children every single day. As a parent who is familiar with NLP, you will have a toolbox of skills and techniques that will help you not only to help them, but to help yourself, too.

From NLP, you will learn how to tap into your child's learning and communication style; this will help you to speak with and teach your children, from a very early age, in the way that they will adapt to the easiest. We each have our own preferences, and when you can identify the learning and communication style for your child, they will be more successful and you will be able to communicate much more easily.

You will also learn skills to build rapport and group cohesion. Just because you live in the same house doesn't mean you have rapport, especially as your children grow into adolescents! Having rapport as a way of beginning any communication, verbal or non-verbal, will help you to open and maintain a strong, loving and supportive connection with your children.

Deliberate questioning skills are taught in NLP so you can gently ask questions and get answers other than, "I don't know" or "nothing," as many kids are prone to give. Our minds are automatically distorting, deleting, and generalising information to make it fit into our schema of the world. The questions from NLP will allow you to uncover what has been distorted, deleted, and generalised, helping your child to widen their scope of understanding, assisting them to make decisions, encouraging them to think outside the square, and to challenge any un-resourceful thoughts of their own.

Plus, NLP is full of tools and techniques to help foster confidence, strength, personal power, and so many more wonderful resources. You will be learning how to motivate and encourage your children based on their unconscious filters, known as Meta-Programs. Throughout all of this, they learn how to be self-responsive, responsible, resourceful, and resilient to anything life brings to them.

We have found over the years that our students who incorporate NLP into their parenting have stronger and more capable children than they had before. After all, as a parent, you are not just a role model; you are also a life coach.

148. Become a Better Trainer

As trainers ourselves, we may be a bit biased when it comes to being a better trainer by incorporating NLP into what we do. But, we do know firsthand the difference it makes as a trainer, to elevate the outcomes of participants and students by training the conscious and unconscious minds.

You see, when you are trained in NLP, you are not only able to understand others better, but you are also able to communicate your message more accurately, too. When we talk about using NLP to train, we actually mean incorporating NLP tools of communication, persuasion, and understanding to deliver a message to a group of people, in a way that will fit best for each of them.

This includes some amazing NLP tools, including identifying and using the learning style of your participants, incorporating specific sensory specific words and phrases to engage your participants at different stages of the learning process, and ensuring that your non-verbal language meets the verbal message you are delivering. This includes your gestures, facial expressions, tempo, tone, and volume of your voice, plus how you are standing, breathing, and even moving.

Additionally, with NLP you will learn how to include metaphors as teaching tools, how to use nested metaphors for more impact, how to create group rapport and cohesion tools, plus how to utilise Ericksonain language for a more impactful message. The list continues; you will learn how to identify and use the unconscious filters of your learners and craft your message to include aspects of many of them at the same time.

NLP considers a wide range of unconscious awareness elements, that when packaged together will help you to be a more well-rounded and robust trainer who can train at both the conscious and unconscious levels of learning. You already know that not everyone learns the same; therefore, no one should be trained the same. Regardless if you are training one-on-one or in a group setting, the skills of NLP will raise your training skills head and shoulders above the rest and ensure your training and learners are capturing as much of your content as possible.

149. Become a Better Manager

If you are a manager, we have a simple question for you: how did you learn to be a manager? If your company or workplace provided you managerial training, they are leaps and bounds ahead of other places. Most people get promoted to a managerial position because they have worked toward that position, and often because they are the next in line. Often, managers don't really possess qualities or skills of a manager but they are the candidate who was chosen.

Regardless if you are already a great manager, new to management, forced to manage, or aspire to manage others, the skills of NLP will help you step up your game.

When you learn NLP, you will be learning the ultimate interpersonal communication skills; communication is often where there is a skills gap when it comes to management. Sure, people talk and give instructions and provide feedback, but is it provided in a way that is useful for the individual?

You see, each of us filters information in a different way. Some people need instructions given in a procedural manner while others require more of an options focus; some people need to see what is required, others need to hear it, and there are those who need hands-on experience before they understand something.

There is a great quote for communication which applies equally as well for managing: *"First seek to understand and then to be understood."* When you can understand how a person filters or makes sense of information, you can then communicate in a way that best suits that individual, therefore helping them to understand your message or instructions more successfully.

As a manager, you will also want to lead, inspire, and motivate your team to do their best job in the most efficient manner. You will learn a variety of tools to help you to build rapport, ask questions, set goals, identify strategies, and even to create and use anchors to access useful and resourceful states or moods.

For team cohesion, you will learn tools about how to build group rapport, understand each other's values, respect each other's models of the world and identify strengths and skill-gaps to cross train and help your staff grow.

Additionally, when you learn NLP you will also learn to identify patterns for yourself that are useful and can be modelled for other areas of life or expanded upon; you'll also identify patterns of belief, behaviour, emotion, and thought that may be barriers to your personal success. You'll also gain skills to boost your confidence, motivation, self-belief, and anything else you need to be the best manager you can be.

There isn't one area of business or managing people that NLP can't assist with. Where will you use your new NLP skills first?

150. Become a Better Friend

Are you a good friend? Of course, your answer will be largely dependent on your definition of what a good friend is.

Some people have an easier time making and maintaining friendships than others. When we work with people to build social skills and relationship skills, we don't often talk about the friends they are making; rather, we examine their own contribution to the dynamics of a friendship. After all, it is a person's behaviour that is often the most important, simply because behaviour is observable and gives us an insight into a person's beliefs, attitudes, resources, and self-concept.

Once you learn NLP, you can change any unresourceful behaviours, beliefs, capabilities, and even your identity as a friend. This might be useful if you find you are too clingy or dependent, or if you are too distant, standoffish, or you don't let yourself be vulnerable.

An article by *Psychology Today* identified a few traits essential for friendship. NLP will help you to identify these traits within yourself, enhance them, or change how they come across to others. Some of these traits include: trustworthy/honest, caring/empathy, confident, supportive, and loyal.

If a person is lacking any of these traits, they may find it challenging to keep long-term relationships. If there is a sense of distrust, a lack of honesty, or a sense that the other person doesn't care, the friendship may seem very one-sided.

Interestingly, by the age of 21, most of our abilities, beliefs, and social skills have been developed. Specifically, developmental psychologist Morris Massey identified the ages of 13-21 to be the socialisation period. It is during this timeframe that you learn how to be a friend, develop empathy, mature your confidence, and relate a level of trustworthiness. If, however, you didn't have a good role model when you were younger, if trust was an issue within your family, or you didn't have an adequate socialisation period, this may account for some deficit in the friendship traits.

We've often found that people who care too much or give too much advice enable their friend's disruptive behaviours, or give too much of themselves away. They also have beliefs about being liked or desires of being wanted equalling what they can give others.

We've also found that people who are dependent on others tend to push friends away, and this sometimes stems into abandonment or other events that may have happened as a young child.

When you learn NLP, not only will you learn tools to build a stronger level of rapport, great skills to understand and communicate more effectively with your friends, you will gain a valuable set of skills that will help you to be truly you. Honesty, integrity, confidence, vulnerability – to just be you. This will also give the room and permission for our friends to simply be themselves too.

When you can take an honest look at the qualities you bring to your friendships, the only real possibility is to become an even better friend.

151. Become a Better Leader

Whenever we train NLP and Leadership workshops, one of the questions we always ask upfront is, "what is the difference between a leader and a manager?" There are usually many different answers, but the most common boils down to: *leaders have people follow them, while managers have people who work for them.*

If you are a business owner with staff or even an exceptional leader, you need to be both a strong leader and manager to get your team on board to follow you towards your vision of success. Leadership is about getting people to understand and believe in your vision and to work with you to achieve your goals, while managing is more about administering and making sure day-to-day activities are happening as they should.

Another question we ask our workshop participants: *"Is leadership a quality that people can learn?"* The overwhelming response we hear is, "Yes."

This is where NLP comes in. NLP is about understanding how the language of your mind creates the patterns that you run. You have patterns or programs for how you do everything; how you get motivated, how you motivate others, how you make decisions, how you communicate, how you achieve your goals. Once you can identify various programs in your life, you can then use NLP to enhance what is working well for you and change what is not.

For example, you might be amazing at giving constructive feedback to your children or friends, but you might have trouble doing the same in the workplace. With NLP, you will be able to identify your personal psychology, including your beliefs, behaviours, and attitudes to model how you give constructive feedback in your personal life so you can do this same thing in the workplace.

You may also have a pattern of self-doubt or self-trust. With NLP, you will learn many tools to help you uncover the root cause for these and change beliefs and behaviours associated to them. Because NLP is working with your unconscious patterns, if there is a desire to make a change in something you do, we can create the programming of your mind to fit your desires.

From an article in *Forbes* Magazine a few years ago, some key characteristics of a strong leader include: honesty and integrity, a strong and dynamic vision, the ability to inspire teams and individuals, the ability to challenge the status quo by pushing the boundaries and thinking outside the box, and exceptional communication skills.

As a leader trained in NLP, you will be heads and shoulders above the rest in your ability to adapt these characteristics into the situation presented to you – whenever and wherever you are.

152. Become a Better Sales Person

Are you a good listener? Are you conscientious, persistent, coachable, respectful, positive, passionate, resilient, personable, and fairly independent?

If so, you will be a great sales person.

According to entrepreneur.com, these are the top qualities of an exceptional sales person. With these traits in abundance, you will be a sales machine, with personal qualities that make you likeable, approachable, and knowledgeable!

If you want to further develop your sales abilities, then NLP will help you!

One thing NLP is known for is modelling excellence. When you know the makeup of an exceptional sales person, you can use your NLP skills to access or create, amplify, and enhance these qualities within yourself.

NLP will also teach you skills to quickly build rapport with anyone, ask questions to truly identify needs, objections and desires, offer tools to identify a person's buying strategy, and even influential language that will speak more directly to your customer or potential customers unconscious mind and needs.

NLP cannot make someone buy something they don't want or need. So, it isn't a manipulation tool or hypnotic sales process. If someone doesn't want to buy something in general, or from you specifically, then they won't. However, if a person is looking for or contemplating a purchase of what your product or service is, by using your NLP skills within your sales approach, you will be more likely to make a sale.

In a recent NLP sales training in Singapore, we conducted a commercial real-estate company, and their sales team increased sales by nearly 40% the quarter after they implemented new NLP strategies within their communication and sales process.

So, when you learn NLP, you will be able to use your new tools in two ways. First, as a set of strategies to help you to personally develop and enhance the qualities of a great sales person. And second, to understand and use the psychology of your customers to sell to them in the way they need to be sold to. When you do this, it won't feel like they are being sold to; instead, they will be selling to themselves.

After all, who really likes to be sold to?

153. Become a Better HR Professional

Many years ago, when I had a real job, I worked in Human Resources Management. I recall a company-wide meeting once where the HR team was accused of not being human and only having resources. When I heard this, I started to understand that our job is a very administration-based one, for the people who work for us. If we were focusing on only the admin.

and missing the people, we were missing a great deal of our role for the company, not to mention job satisfaction for the people on my team.

Unfortunately, this was well before I was trained and skilled in NLP. Now, however, I get the opportunity to train, consult, and coach HR professionals. The most common topic or theme? Communication, interpersonal relationships, managing and motivating, recruiting, and getting the human back into the resources.

As an HR professional, you will come to understand the diversity of your role and the impact you can have on your company—both positively and negatively. As a cost centre for most companies, you may not always have the financial or time support from other departments to access the resources you need to promote positive change and well-being for the company. However, as a team member and person of influence, you can make a positive and proactive change, just by starting with you and the HR team.

The most impact you will be able to have with your NLP skills in human resources is in communication, change management, and recruitment.

A foundational element of NLP is communication and understanding how each person has their individual communication preferences, filters, and beliefs. When you can identify these factors, you have more ability to get your message across with ease. The NLP communication skills take into account verbal, non-verbal, and written communication, allowing you to be a better communicator across all mediums of communication.

A lot of people don't like change because it contains a large element of uncertainty and ambiguity. From your NLP training, you will learn how people filter information though their psychological makeup, and you will then be more effective at helping facilitate change, while leading people through the change in different ways. For example, a person may not like change, but will adapt to it better having some certainty about the process. Another person may get overwhelmed with the details of the change, so more of a big-picture approach may be needed.

Finally, recruitment is a key aspect of many HR departments. Unfortunately, too much of the recruitment is being outsourced these days, which can create a communication gap. However, if your company still works with recruitment, there are amazing tools that better ensure the right candidate secures your jobs. You will learn dynamic tools like building rapport, watching eye-accessing cues to identify where people are accessing stored memories from, questioning techniques that will allow you to go below the surface to gain a better understanding about the candidates unconscious processing, values based interviewing to find out what truly is important to a person for career success, and most importantly, you will be able to work with managers to identify what psychological mindsets are required for success and profile candidates according to the needs of the role and company.

Personally, you will also benefit from learning NLP. All the skills and tools that you'll learn can be easily applied to your own personal life as well in the business world. When you can step into NLP as a personal growth tool, you will also learn how to better communicate and manage yourself.

Isn't it time to put the human back into your resources and get the most job satisfaction and the best results you can for yourself, your team and your company?

154. Become a Better Teacher

As a teacher, you probably have a passion for making a difference to the lives of others, regardless of the age of your pupils. By using NLP in your classroom, you will be able to facilitate your students learning more effectively, even leaving a long-term impact of you and the lessons you have shared.

Teaching isn't simply about imparting information so a test can be taken; it is a part of a larger element of education. Possibly one of the most important elements of education is helping students to develop a strong sense of self, self-esteem, and self-confidence.

When you learn NLP, and incorporate these skills into the classroom, you will not only communicate and teach your subject matter more elegantly to your student's unconscious awareness, but you will also be impacting them positively in many ways.

In addition to amazing tools such as identifying and using your students preferred learning style, being able to ask more effective questions, developing sensory acuity skills to recognize when learning 'fits' or not, you will have a toolbox of so many other skills.

Many teachers blend NLP skills like setting **Resource Anchors** with their students to anchor, or trigger the classroom environment to be a positive experience, boost the morale of the students, and to establish a sense of safety to learn and make mistakes.

By learning how to communicate in an influential manner, you will also be able to identify and use the best learning strategies of your students, identify how they best take in and retain information and how they are most effectively motivated. You will be able to ascertain how to encourage, praise, reprimand, coach, and inspire each student in the way they need.

From lesson planning, creating anchors, using sensory learning, non-verbal cues, and so much more, there are so many ways to include NLP in your classroom. Not only will you enjoy the teaching process more, your students will be delighted with NLP being used in the classroom to help them bloom!

155. Become a Better Health Professional

Throughout the world, health professionals are known for a lack of bedside manner, for doling out drugs, and for looking for a diagnosis rather than aiming for a cure. Now, we know not all health professionals fit into this broad generalisation, but enough do that more and more people are turning to alternative medicines and practices.

From an NLP perspective, we know that the mind and body are connected and therefore affect each other.

We have trained hundreds of health professionals, medical doctors, surgeons, dentists, counsellors, psychologists, and even psychiatrists in NLP, and their feedback states they now have tools to treat patients in a more holistic manner.

One of our students is a medical doctor in an emergency room. One of her complaints about her job is that she didn't get enough time to spend with patients to offer them a kind word; she instead was focused on figuring out what was wrong with the patient as quickly as possible and often missing out on key criteria because of this rush.

Post learning NLP, she reported that in the same amount of time, she could build rapport, question the patient, and ascertain the problem and route to a solution much more effectively.

General practitioners, counsellors, and psychologists tell us that they spend more time building rapport, identifying not just the problem but the desired state of their patients, thus providing more efficient treatment. Counsellors and psychologists also incorporate more of the NLP tools to help identify and clear unresourceful patterns such as emotions, beliefs, behaviours, and negative thinking.

NLP even has processes that work with the mind body connection to communicate with the symptoms of an illness, pain, emotion, or disease to identify what is needed in the way of a change or the development of resources.

As a health professional with NLP, you will be more equipped to better understand your patients, both consciously and unconsciously.

156. Become a Better Personal Trainer

As a Personal Trainer, your role is compacted with many others and as a result you need to be more responsible in serving your clients in the best possible way. To your clients, you are more than just a trainer. You are their confidant, nurse, therapist, advisor, educator, role model, motivator, and overall guide. You serve as an inspiration and often someone to aspire to. Your clients treat you as a trustworthy friend, and you need to ensure they are **modelling excellence.**

First and foremost, when you learn NLP, you will apply the skills and tools to yourself, uncovering any limits, barriers, or blocks you may have while building and accessing resources to help you on your journey. This will put you in the clients' shoes so to speak; experiencing the positive gains from NLP techniques and processes will provide the confidence and understanding of how to apply it to others. After all, personal trainers trained in NLP can help clients with their mindset faster and permanently, which helps clients achieve their goals.

Three of the immediate tools from NLP you will implement with your clients are rapport, sensory acuity, and questioning techniques.

NLP will help facilitate a change in your client's mindset and psychology, and is strengthened first by creating a stabilizing a relationship with strong **rapport**. Rapport allows people to open to you so they feel truly heard.

From there, you will use a variety of **meta model questions** that are specifically designed to communicate with the unconscious mind and uncover what has been distorted, deleted, and generalised; this will help you to ask better questions to get to the core of your clients' desired goals and blocks that have held them back in the past. You will also learn an exquisite goal setting tool called the **well-formed outcome**, which will encapsulate your client's needs, desires, blocks, and resources.

While working with your clients, at any stage of your work together, it is important to develop a strong **sensory acuity** to notice their physiology, eye patterns, language, and representational systems to gain deeper understanding of what makes your client tick. These skills provide more insight into the 'true' nature of what the clients are really saying, trying to communicate, or in some instances trying *not* to communicate.

Being able to address poor choices and unconscious conditioning is imperative for long-term success of your clients. Therefore, you will have a toolbox of beneficial NLP processes and techniques to identify and remove limiting beliefs, negative emotions, unresourceful patterns, negative thinking, sabotaging behaviors, and more.

Additionally, with NLP you will learn many **anchoring** techniques that will help your clients change their state, mood or emotion in an instant. This can help your client find more motivation, drive, determination, and willpower to succeed.

Of course, these are just a handful of NLP processes that will help you put "personal" back into personal training. For your training business, you'll be able to assist your client in more ways than just training. We all know that your client's success is the best advertisement!

Now What?

You may have picked up this book with a mild curiosity, but we hope that has shifted into a roaring flame of intrigue. As we have shown you through this book, there is not one aspect of life that cannot be benefitted from NLP.

You may be asking yourself, "Now what!? I want more!"

If so, we have done our job.

We would now like to invite you to continue your journey learning more about NLP, and not just surface information about how NLP will benefit you, but really learning the tools, strategies, and concepts that will fully put you into the drivers seat of life.

As you have learned, you are in charge of your mind and therefore your results. You have been introduced to so many NLP skills that we want to empower you with knowing and learning at a cellular level. Getting hands-on experience with the tools of NLP will help you to be the best version of yourself. No more excuses—you now know how NLP can upskill your life to the next level.

If we could make learning a prerequisite to parenting, leading, managing, teaching, or just becoming an adult, we would. The world would be a much better place if everyone were skilled in NLP.

For readers of this book, we have a special webpage set up with more information about NLP and learning NLP, please join us at: **www.youmustlearnnlp. com/now-what**

As a starting place, we encourage you to do the following (not in any particular order):

1. **Complete an NLP Practitioner Training course:** You can find our upcoming trainings at nlpworldwide.com. Even if we don't train in your part of the world, we have students that travel around the globe to learn with us. This is a 7 or 8-day in-person program

that will teach you the fundamentals and foundational knowledge about NLP, including everything from rapport, meta questions, and metaprograms, to anchoring, submodalities, timeline, parts integration, Ericksonian hypnosis and so many other tools you heard about in this book are covered in the training.

2. **Read our book *30 Days to NLP*:** This is our Introduction to NLP text book we wrote and use in our NLP trainings. You can buy it online as a paperback or electronic version on Amazon or at www.30daystonlp.com

3. **Join our online training with anywherenlp.com:** If you can't get to us live, online will be the next-best thing. Although this is not a certification training, you will learn the same fundamental concepts in the live training, just without the practical application or group.

4. **Connect with our online introduction to NLP:** Our online introduction will offer you more insights into us, the history of NLP, your three minds, and the presuppositions of NLP.

5. **Use our coaching services:** Laureli and Heidi and our team work with clients one-on-one or in group settings with NLP. If you are interested in getting your own personal or business coaching or therapy.

Links to everything above, plus more videos and articles can be found at **www.youmustlearnnlp.com/now-what**

We cannot emphasise enough the practical benefits of learning NLP in an interactive environment where you can safely try all the skills, clear your personal interferences, and build resources you need to better communicate, lead, manage, and live. Many parents and business professionals appreciate the concentrated structure of our training with the 7 or 8-day format with ample opportunity to learn the skills, clear your own interferences, grow personally, and embody NLP.

Thank you for taking the time out of your life to find out more about how NLP will befit your life. We look forward to another opportunity where we can share even more of our world of NLP with you soon.

Contact Us Anytime

We are always grateful to connect with like-mined people on a journey for personal growth, and its especially great to hear from people who have read our books, seen our videos or have attended workshops. So, if you have any questions or would just like to say hello, send an email to us at **info@ nlpworldwide.com** and send us a message. We look forward to hearing from you, and exploring how we can help you to further explore NLP in our life.

Help Us Help Others

Can we ask you a quick favour?

If you feel this book has given you more insight into NLP, the value learning NLP can add to your life, and if you can think of anyone else who might benefit from our message, I'm hoping you'll do something for someone else:

Give this book to them. Or let them borrow your copy. Or better yet, get them their own copy as a gift. They can also purchase their own at **www. youmustlearnnlp.com**

If you believe, as we do, that NLP is worth sharing with more people in this world, please help us to share it though this book.

Thank you so much.

NLP Presuppositions

In NLP, presuppositions are simply assumptions that NLP is based on. They can be used as filters in life or in NLP. We have highlighted just a few presuppositions here, however over 80 different presuppositions of NLP exist:

1. The meaning of communication is the response you get.
2. The map is not the territory.
3. The Law of Requisite Variety: The system/person with the most flexibility of behaviour will control the system.
4. People are doing the best they can with the resources they have available.
5. People have all the resources they need to succeed and to achieve their desired outcomes.
6. Respect for the other person's model of the world.
7. Every behaviour has a positive intention.
8. The most important information about a person is that person's behaviour.
9. People are not their behaviours.
10. You are in charge of your mind and therefore your results.
11. There is no failure, only feedback.
12. Resistance in communication is a sign of a lack of rapport.
13. All procedures should increase choice and wholeness.
14. The mind and body are connected and therefore affect each other.
15. When you know better you can do better.
16. Everyone has the potential for genius.

NLP Tools for Communication

- Representational System
- Calibration/Sensory Acuity
- Rapport
- Meta Programs
- Reframing
- Metaphors
- Indirect Suggestions
- Use Submodalities
- Use Strategies
- Meta Model
- Eye Accessing Cues
- Chunking Up/Down
- Elicit Values/Beliefs
- Elicit Strategies
- State Elicitation
- Elicit Submodalities
- Perceptual Positions
- Elicit Timeline
- Test and Future Pace
- Client Summary
- Well-Formed Outcome
- Sleight of Mouth Patterns

NLP Techniques for Clearing Interferences and Accessing Resources

- Congruence
- Meta Model
- State Management
- Resource Anchor
- Circle of Excellence
- Chunking up/down
- Integrating Anchors
- Understanding Strategy
- Presuppositions
- Milton Model
- Well Formed Outcome
- Enhance Submodalities
- Perceptual Positions Exercise
- Metaphor
- Reframing
- Communicate with Symptoms
- Parts Integration
- Unconscious Pattern Change
- Clear Anxiety and Worry
- Neurological Levels Alignment
- Collapsing Anchors
- Clearing the Now
- Change Timeline
- Change Submodalities
- VK Dissociation
- Indirect Suggestions
- Auditory Perspective
- Visual Perspective
- Change Personal History
- Reimprinting
- Tunnelling
- Disney Planning Process
- Mapping Across Meta Programs
- Drop Down Through
- Clean Language
- Meta Stating Concepts
- Depleasuring Process
- Sacred Journey
- Foreground Background
- Neuro Repair Change
- Clearing the Now
- Swish Pattern
- Changing Values
- Core Transformation
- New Behaviour Generator